MINDFULNESS TECHNIQUES FOR THE BUSY PROFESSIONAL

Unlocking Focus, Balance, and Success in Today's Fast-Paced Workplace

Edan Seaton

CONTENTS

Title Page
Chapter 1: Introduction to Mindfulness for the Modern Professional ... 1
Chapter 2: The Busy Professional's Dilemma ... 9
Chapter 3: Mindful Breathing: Your Anchor in the Storm ... 20
Chapter 4: Mindful Body Awareness: Tuning into Your Physical Self ... 29
Chapter 5: Mindful Eating: Nourishing Body and Mind ... 39
Chapter 6: Mindful Communication: Enhancing Professional Relationships ... 49
Chapter 7: Mindful Time Management: Doing More by Doing Less ... 59
Chapter 8: Mindful Decision Making: Clarity in the Face of Complexity ... 67
Chapter 9: Mindfulness for Leadership: Cultivating Presence and Vision ... 75
Chapter 10: Digital Mindfulness: Navigating the Always-On World ... 85
Chapter 11: Creating Your Personalized Mindfulness Practice ... 95
Chapter 12: The Mindful Professional: Putting It All Together ... 105

CHAPTER 1: INTRODUCTION TO MINDFULNESS FOR THE MODERN PROFESSIONAL

In today's fast-paced, hyper-connected world, professionals are constantly bombarded with information, deadlines, and demands. The pressure to perform, innovate, and succeed can be overwhelming, often leading to stress, burnout, and a diminished quality of life. Amidst this chaotic landscape, a powerful tool has emerged, offering a pathway to clarity, focus, and well-being: mindfulness.
The modern workplace is characterized by a relentless pace and ever-increasing expectations. Professionals are expected to juggle multiple projects, respond to an endless stream of emails, attend back-to-back meetings, and stay ahead of rapidly evolving industry trends. This constant state of high alert can lead to chronic stress, which not only affects our mental and physical health but also impairs our ability to perform at our best.
Moreover, the boundaries between work and personal life have

become increasingly blurred, especially with the rise of remote work and digital connectivity. Many professionals find themselves "always on," checking emails late into the night or ruminating about work issues during family time. This lack of clear separation can lead to a sense of imbalance and dissatisfaction in both professional and personal spheres.

Mindfulness, at its core, is the practice of being fully present and engaged in the current moment, aware of our thoughts, feelings, and surroundings without judgment. It's a state of active, open attention to the present. This simple yet profound concept has roots in ancient Buddhist meditation practices but has gained significant traction in recent years as a secular approach to managing the complexities of modern life.

The origins of mindfulness can be traced back over 2,500 years to the teachings of the Buddha. However, its modern, secular application in the West began in the late 1970s with the work of Jon Kabat-Zinn, who developed Mindfulness-Based Stress Reduction (MBSR) at the University of Massachusetts Medical Center. Since then, mindfulness has been adapted and applied in various contexts, from healthcare and education to business and sports.

In the professional context, mindfulness offers a way to cultivate mental clarity, emotional balance, and resilience in the face of workplace challenges. It provides tools to manage stress, enhance focus, and improve interpersonal relationships. By training our attention and awareness, we can develop the capacity to respond to work situations with greater skill and less reactivity.

For the busy professional, mindfulness offers a respite from the constant mental chatter and external pressures that can dominate our workdays. It provides a way to step back from the endless to-do lists, the cascade of emails, and the persistent buzz of notifications, allowing us to reconnect with ourselves and approach our work with renewed focus and clarity.

One of the key benefits of mindfulness for professionals is its ability to enhance our capacity for focused attention. In a world of constant distractions, the ability to concentrate deeply on a task is becoming increasingly rare and valuable. Mindfulness training helps us recognize when our mind has wandered and gently bring our attention back to the present moment, strengthening our "attention muscle" over time.

Furthermore, mindfulness can help us manage the cognitive overload that many professionals experience. By practicing present-moment awareness, we can learn to process information more efficiently, prioritize more effectively, and make clearer decisions. This can lead to improved productivity and a greater sense of control over our workload.

The science behind mindfulness is compelling. Numerous studies have shown that regular mindfulness practice can lead to significant changes in both the structure and function of the brain. Neuroscientists have observed increased gray matter density in brain regions associated with learning, memory, emotional regulation, and perspective-taking in individuals who practice mindfulness regularly. These physical changes in the brain correlate with improvements in cognitive function, emotional stability, and overall well-being.

Research using functional magnetic resonance imaging (fMRI) has shown that mindfulness meditation can reduce activity in the amygdala, the brain's "fight or flight" center, and increase connectivity between the amygdala and prefrontal cortex. This suggests that mindfulness can help us respond more skillfully to stressful situations, rather than reacting automatically.

Studies have also found that mindfulness practice can lead to changes in gene expression, potentially influencing how our cells respond to stress. This emerging field of research, known as epigenetics, suggests that mindfulness may have far-reaching effects on our physical health and resilience.

For professionals, the benefits of mindfulness are particularly relevant. Research has demonstrated that mindfulness can enhance focus and concentration, improve decision-making skills, boost creativity, and increase resilience to stress. It can also lead to better emotional intelligence, which is crucial for effective leadership and teamwork. Moreover, mindfulness has been shown to enhance overall job satisfaction and work-life balance, contributing to both personal happiness and professional success. In the realm of leadership, mindfulness has been associated with improved emotional intelligence, better decision-making under pressure, and enhanced ability to inspire and motivate teams. Mindful leaders tend to be more self-aware, empathetic, and adaptable – qualities that are increasingly valued in today's complex and rapidly changing business environment.

For individual contributors, mindfulness can enhance problem-solving skills, creativity, and the ability to collaborate effectively with others. It can also help manage work-related anxiety and imposter syndrome, allowing professionals to approach challenges with greater confidence and clarity.

Despite its growing popularity, there are still many misconceptions about mindfulness. Some view it as a time-consuming practice that requires hours of meditation or retreat from the world. Others see it as a form of religious practice or dismiss it as New Age fluff. In reality, mindfulness is a practical, evidence-based approach that can be integrated into even the busiest of schedules. It doesn't require any special equipment or environment, and its principles can be applied to virtually any aspect of professional life.

One common misconception is that mindfulness is about emptying the mind or achieving a state of constant calm. In fact, mindfulness is about developing a different relationship with our thoughts and emotions – observing them without getting caught up in them. It's not about suppressing or eliminating thoughts, but rather about learning to respond to them more skillfully.

Another myth is that mindfulness is incompatible with ambition or high performance. On the contrary, many high-achieving professionals and athletes use mindfulness to enhance their focus, manage pressure, and perform at their best. Mindfulness can actually sharpen our ability to pursue goals effectively, by helping us stay present and engaged in the process rather than getting lost in worry about the future or rumination about the past.

This book aims to demystify mindfulness and provide busy professionals with practical, accessible techniques to incorporate mindfulness into their daily lives. We'll explore a range of mindfulness practices, from brief breathing exercises that can be done at your desk to more comprehensive strategies for mindful communication, decision-making, and leadership.

Our approach is grounded in both scientific research and practical application. We'll draw on the latest findings from neuroscience, psychology, and organizational behavior to explain how and why mindfulness works. At the same time, we'll provide concrete, actionable strategies that you can implement immediately in your professional life.

Throughout the chapters that follow, we'll delve into specific areas where mindfulness can have a profound impact on your professional life. We'll start by examining the unique challenges faced by modern professionals and how mindfulness can address these issues. From there, we'll explore foundational mindfulness techniques such as mindful breathing and body awareness, before moving on to more specific applications like mindful eating, communication, and time management.

We'll explore how mindfulness can enhance your ability to focus and manage your attention effectively. You'll learn techniques for staying present and engaged during meetings, managing multiple projects without feeling overwhelmed, and transitioning smoothly between different tasks throughout your day.

We'll also dive into the role of mindfulness in managing workplace stress and building resilience. You'll discover practices for staying grounded in high-pressure situations, managing difficult emotions, and maintaining a sense of balance even in the face of challenging deadlines or conflicts.

The book will also cover mindfulness-based approaches to enhancing creativity and innovation. We'll explore how mindfulness can help you tap into your creative potential, overcome mental blocks, and approach problem-solving with fresh perspectives.

We'll look at how mindfulness can enhance higher-level professional skills such as decision-making and leadership, and how it can help navigate the digital landscape that dominates much of modern work life. You'll learn how to use mindfulness to make more balanced, insightful decisions, and how to lead with greater presence and emotional intelligence.

In our exploration of mindful leadership, we'll discuss how mindfulness can enhance your ability to inspire and motivate others, navigate complex organizational dynamics, and create a more positive and productive work environment. We'll also look at how mindful leadership practices can contribute to building more ethical, sustainable organizations.

The book will also address the challenges of maintaining mindfulness in our increasingly digital world. We'll explore strategies for managing email overload, practicing digital detox, and using technology mindfully to support rather than hinder our well-being and productivity.

Finally, we'll guide you in creating a personalized mindfulness practice that fits your unique needs and lifestyle. This will include tips for integrating mindfulness into your daily routine, overcoming common obstacles to practice, and gradually expanding your mindfulness skills over time.

The goal of this book is not to add another item to your to-do list or to suggest that you need to dramatically overhaul your life. Instead, we aim to provide you with a toolkit of mindfulness techniques that you can seamlessly integrate into your existing routine. These practices are designed to help you work smarter, not harder, by cultivating a greater sense of presence, focus, and clarity in your professional life.

We recognize that every professional's journey is unique, and what works for one person may not work for another. That's why we'll offer a variety of techniques and approaches throughout the book, encouraging you to experiment and find what resonates most with you. The key is to approach mindfulness with an attitude of curiosity and openness, rather than as another task to perfect or achieve.

As you progress through this book, remember that mindfulness is a skill that develops over time. Like any skill, it requires practice and patience. There may be times when it feels challenging or when you struggle to maintain consistency. This is normal and part of the learning process. The key is to approach your mindfulness practice with an attitude of curiosity and non-judgment, allowing yourself to explore and experiment with different techniques to find what works best for you.

It's important to note that the benefits of mindfulness are cumulative. While you may experience some immediate effects, such as feeling calmer after a brief meditation, the most profound changes often occur gradually over time. Consistency in practice, even if it's just a few minutes a day, is more important than long, sporadic sessions.

By the end of this book, you'll have a comprehensive understanding of how mindfulness can transform your professional life, along with a practical set of tools to implement these concepts in your daily routine. Whether you're a seasoned executive, an entrepreneur, or an emerging professional, the mindfulness techniques presented here can help you navigate the challenges of modern work life with greater ease, effectiveness, and satisfaction.

You'll have strategies for managing stress, enhancing focus, improving communication, making better decisions, and leading with greater presence and emotional intelligence. More importantly, you'll have developed a new way of relating to your work and to yourself – one characterized by greater awareness, balance, and intentionality.

So, let's begin this journey towards becoming a more mindful professional. As we explore the various facets of mindfulness in the workplace, keep an open mind and be willing to challenge some of your existing habits and perspectives. Remember, mindfulness is not about achieving a perfect state of calm or eliminating all stress from your life. It's about developing a different relationship with your experiences – one that allows you to respond more skillfully to whatever arises in your work and life.

The path to a more mindful professional life starts here, with each moment of awareness you bring to your work and to yourself. As you turn the page to the next chapter, take a deep breath and set an intention for your mindfulness journey. What do you hope to gain from this exploration? How might greater mindfulness enhance your professional life? With these questions in mind, let's dive deeper into the world of mindfulness for the modern professional.

CHAPTER 2: THE BUSY PROFESSIONAL'S DILEMMA

In today's fast-paced professional world, busyness has become a badge of honor. We wear our packed schedules and endless to-do lists like armor, equating our worth with our productivity. This culture of busyness has permeated every aspect of our working lives, creating a relentless cycle of stress, burnout, and diminished well-being. As we dive into this chapter, we'll explore the unique challenges faced by modern professionals and how mindfulness can offer a powerful antidote to these issues.

The origins of this "cult of busyness" can be traced back to the Industrial Revolution, where time became commodified and productivity became the measure of an individual's value. This mindset has only intensified in the digital age, where the boundaries between work and personal life have become increasingly blurred. The result is a work culture that often prioritizes quantity over quality, speed over thoughtfulness, and constant action over strategic reflection.

This shift has profound implications for how we perceive ourselves and our worth in the professional world. Many of us have internalized the belief that being busy equates to being important or successful. We fear that if we're not constantly engaged in work-related activities, we'll fall behind or be perceived as less committed than our peers. This fear drives us to take on more tasks, extend our working hours, and sacrifice personal time in the pursuit of professional advancement.

The culture of busyness is not just a personal phenomenon; it's a societal shift that has redefined our relationship with work. We live in an era where being "busy" is often conflated with being important or successful. This mindset has led to a work environment where constant activity is prized over thoughtful action, where quantity of output often overshadows quality. The impact of this culture on our well-being is profound and far-reaching.

One of the most insidious aspects of this culture is the way it normalizes overwork and stress. When everyone around us is working long hours and constantly talking about how busy they are, it becomes the expected norm. This normalization makes it difficult for individuals to recognize when they're pushing themselves too hard or to justify taking time for rest and self-care.

Moreover, the culture of busyness often leads to a state of continuous partial attention. We find ourselves constantly multitasking, jumping from one task to another without ever fully engaging with any single activity. This fragmented attention not only reduces our effectiveness but also leaves us feeling scattered and unfulfilled, even after a long day of work.

Stress has become an almost ubiquitous feature of professional life. The American Psychological Association's annual Stress in America survey consistently finds that work is one of the top sources of stress for adults. This chronic stress takes a toll on both our physical and mental health. It can lead to a host of health problems, including cardiovascular disease, weakened immune system, and mental health issues such as anxiety and depression.

The physiological impact of chronic work-related stress is significant. When we're constantly in a state of high alert, our bodies produce elevated levels of stress hormones like cortisol and adrenaline. Over time, this can lead to a range of health issues, including high blood pressure, digestive problems, and compromised immune function. Additionally, chronic stress can affect our sleep patterns, leading to insomnia or poor sleep quality, which further exacerbates health problems and reduces our ability to cope with work demands.

Furthermore, the psychological toll of constant stress can be equally devastating. Prolonged exposure to work-related stress can lead to anxiety disorders, depression, and other mental health issues. It can also contribute to cognitive problems, including difficulty concentrating, memory issues, and reduced problem-solving abilities – all of which can significantly impact our professional performance.

Moreover, prolonged exposure to high levels of stress often results in burnout. Burnout is characterized by emotional exhaustion, cynicism, and a reduced sense of personal accomplishment. It's a state of physical, emotional, and mental exhaustion that occurs when we experience long-term stress in our jobs. The World Health Organization has recognized burnout as an occupational phenomenon, highlighting its prevalence and impact in the modern workplace.

Burnout is more than just feeling tired or stressed; it's a state of complete emotional and physical depletion. Individuals experiencing burnout often feel a sense of detachment from their work, a loss of motivation, and a decreased sense of personal accomplishment. This can lead to reduced job performance, increased absenteeism, and higher turnover rates, which not only affect the individual but also have significant implications for organizations as a whole.

The progression from stress to burnout is often gradual, making it difficult for individuals to recognize the signs before reaching a crisis point. It typically begins with a period of high idealism and commitment, where an individual pours excessive time and energy into their work. Over time, as the demands of the job outweigh the rewards, feelings of frustration and fatigue begin to set in. If not addressed, this can lead to a state of cynicism and detachment, ultimately resulting in full-blown burnout.

The effects of stress and burnout on productivity are significant. While we may think that working longer hours and pushing ourselves to the limit will result in greater output, research suggests otherwise. Studies have shown that prolonged periods of stress actually decrease productivity, impair decision-making, and reduce creativity. In essence, the very culture that prizes busyness may be undermining the results it seeks to achieve.

Research in cognitive psychology has demonstrated that our brains are not designed for the kind of constant, high-intensity focus that the culture of busyness demands. Our cognitive resources are limited, and without adequate periods of rest and recovery, our ability to concentrate, make decisions, and think creatively diminishes significantly. This means that beyond a certain point, working longer hours doesn't lead to increased productivity – instead, it leads to diminishing returns and increased errors.

Furthermore, chronic stress and burnout can lead to a phenomenon known as "presenteeism," where employees are physically present at work but not fully functioning due to health issues or lack of engagement. Presenteeism can be even more costly to organizations than absenteeism, as it results in reduced productivity without the obvious signal of an empty desk.

Technology, while offering numerous benefits to the modern professional, has also contributed significantly to our culture of busyness. The advent of smartphones, email, and instant messaging has created an "always-on" work culture. We're expected to be available and responsive at all hours, blurring the lines between work and personal time. This constant connectivity leads to increased distraction and fragmented attention, making it difficult to focus deeply on any single task.

The ubiquity of digital devices means that work is always just a tap or click away. This constant availability can create a sense of urgency around every notification, making it difficult to fully disconnect from work even during personal time. The result is a state of continuous partial attention, where we're never fully engaged in work or fully present in our personal lives.

Moreover, the sheer volume of information we're exposed to through digital channels can be overwhelming. We're constantly bombarded with emails, messages, news updates, and social media notifications, all competing for our attention. This information overload can lead to decision fatigue and reduced cognitive capacity, further contributing to stress and burnout.

The ping of a new email or the buzz of a text message triggers a dopamine release in our brains, creating a cycle of constant checking and interruption. This not only reduces our productivity but also increases our stress levels as we feel perpetually behind and unable to keep up with the influx of information and demands.

This dopamine-driven cycle of notification and response can become addictive, leading to compulsive checking behaviors that further fragment our attention and increase stress. We find ourselves unable to resist the urge to check our devices, even when we know it's disrupting our focus or interfering with our personal time.

Furthermore, the constant influx of new information and tasks can create a sense of perpetual urgency, where everything feels important and time-sensitive. This can lead to difficulty prioritizing tasks and a tendency to focus on immediate, often less important tasks at the expense of longer-term, more significant projects.

In this environment, the need for work-life balance has never been more critical. Yet, ironically, it has also never been more challenging to achieve. The same technology that allows us to work flexibly from anywhere also makes it difficult to truly disconnect from work. Many professionals find themselves checking work emails late into the night or spending weekends catching up on tasks, further eroding the boundaries between work and personal life.

The concept of work-life balance itself has evolved in response to these changes. Rather than a strict separation between work and personal time, many professionals now seek work-life integration, where they can blend professional and personal activities in a way that feels harmonious and fulfilling. However, achieving this integration requires a high level of self-awareness and intentionality, which can be difficult to maintain in the face of constant demands and distractions.

Moreover, the gig economy and the rise of remote work have further blurred the lines between work and personal life. While these changes offer increased flexibility, they also create new challenges in terms of setting boundaries and managing time effectively. Without the physical separation of a workplace, it can be even more difficult to "switch off" from work mode.

This lack of balance not only affects our personal relationships and overall life satisfaction but also impacts our professional performance. Without adequate time for rest, relaxation, and pursuits outside of work, we deprive ourselves of the opportunity to recharge and gain new perspectives that can enhance our creativity and problem-solving abilities at work.

Research in neuroscience and psychology has shown that periods of rest and disengagement from work are crucial for cognitive function and creativity. During these periods of "downtime," our brains engage in important processes of consolidation and integration, which are essential for learning, memory formation, and creative problem-solving. By constantly engaging in work-related activities, we rob ourselves of these vital cognitive processes.

Furthermore, a lack of work-life balance can lead to a narrowing of perspective. When we're constantly immersed in work, we can lose touch with other aspects of life that provide meaning, inspiration, and new ideas. This not only affects our personal fulfillment but can also limit our professional growth and innovation.

So, how can mindfulness help address these challenges? At its core, mindfulness offers a way to step back from the constant doing and cultivate a sense of being. It provides tools to manage stress, increase focus, and improve overall well-being, directly addressing many of the issues faced by busy professionals.

Mindfulness practices offer a counterpoint to the culture of busyness by emphasizing presence and awareness over constant activity. By learning to be more fully present in each moment, we can break the cycle of reactivity and compulsive busyness that often drives our work lives. This doesn't mean becoming less productive; rather, it means bringing a quality of attention and intentionality to our work that can actually enhance our effectiveness.

One of the key benefits of mindfulness is its ability to help us discern between truly important tasks and those that merely feel urgent. By cultivating a practice of pausing and bringing awareness to our thoughts and feelings, we can make more conscious choices about how we allocate our time and energy. This can lead to a more strategic and fulfilling approach to our work.

Firstly, mindfulness practices can help reduce stress by activating the body's relaxation response. Regular mindfulness meditation has been shown to lower cortisol levels (the stress hormone) and reduce activity in the amygdala, the brain's fear center. This can lead to a greater sense of calm and resilience in the face of work pressures.

The relaxation response, first described by Dr. Herbert Benson, is the physiological opposite of the stress response. When activated through mindfulness practices, it leads to decreased heart rate, lowered blood pressure, and reduced muscle tension. Over time, regular activation of the relaxation response can help to counteract the harmful effects of chronic stress on the body and mind.

Moreover, mindfulness practices have been shown to increase activity in the prefrontal cortex, the area of the brain responsible for executive function, emotional regulation, and decision-making. This enhanced prefrontal cortex function can lead to improved emotional regulation and more effective stress management in the workplace.

Mindfulness also enhances our ability to focus and resist distractions. By training our attention through mindfulness practices, we can become more adept at staying on task and avoiding the constant pull of emails, messages, and other interruptions. This improved focus can lead to greater productivity and more satisfying work experiences.

The ability to sustain attention is like a muscle that can be strengthened through mindfulness practice. Regular meditation has been shown to increase the density of gray matter in brain regions associated with learning, memory, and emotional regulation. This neuroplasticity means that we can actually reshape our brains to become more focused and resilient in the face of distractions.

Furthermore, mindfulness can help us develop metacognition – the ability to observe our own thought processes. This skill allows us to notice when our mind has wandered and bring it back to the task at hand, a crucial ability in our distraction-filled work environments.

Moreover, mindfulness can help us cultivate a greater awareness of our thoughts, emotions, and physical sensations. This awareness allows us to recognize signs of stress or burnout early, enabling us to take proactive steps to maintain our well-being. It also helps us make more conscious choices about how we spend our time and energy, supporting better work-life balance.

By developing this heightened self-awareness, we can begin to notice patterns in our behavior and emotional responses at work. We might recognize, for instance, that certain types of tasks or interactions tend to drain our energy, while others energize us. This insight can inform how we structure our workday and manage our resources for optimal performance and well-being.

Mindfulness also fosters a non-judgmental attitude towards our experiences, which can be particularly beneficial in high-pressure work environments. Instead of berating ourselves for feeling stressed or anxious, we can acknowledge these feelings with compassion and respond to them more skillfully.

In terms of technology use, mindfulness can help us develop a healthier relationship with our devices. By becoming more aware of our habits and impulses around technology, we can make more intentional choices about when and how we engage with our devices, reducing the sense of being constantly tethered to work.

Mindful technology use might involve setting specific times to check emails rather than responding to every notification, or creating tech-free zones or periods in our day. It could also mean being more conscious of how we use social media and other potentially distracting apps during work hours.

Additionally, mindfulness can help us become more aware of the physical and emotional effects of prolonged device use. We might notice, for instance, how our posture changes or how our stress levels increase after extended screen time. This awareness can prompt us to take regular breaks and engage in activities that counteract the negative effects of technology use.

As we move forward in this book, we'll explore specific mindfulness techniques that address these challenges. We'll learn how to use mindful breathing to manage stress, how to cultivate body awareness to recognize and release tension, and how to apply mindfulness principles to improve our communication, time management, and decision-making skills.

These techniques will provide practical tools for navigating the busy professional's dilemma. For instance, we'll explore how brief mindfulness practices can be integrated into a busy workday, providing moments of calm and clarity without requiring a significant time commitment. We'll also look at how mindfulness can enhance our interactions with colleagues, improving communication and collaboration in high-pressure environments.

We'll delve into mindfulness-based approaches to time management, exploring how greater presence and awareness can help us prioritize tasks more effectively and work with greater focus and efficiency. We'll also examine how mindfulness can support better decision-making, helping us to respond to workplace challenges with greater clarity and wisdom.

The busy professional's dilemma is real, but it's not insurmountable. By incorporating mindfulness into our professional lives, we can begin to shift from a culture of mindless busyness to one of mindful productivity. We can learn to work smarter, not just harder, and to find greater satisfaction and success in our careers without sacrificing our well-being.

This shift towards mindful productivity represents a fundamental change in how we approach our work. It's about moving from a quantity-focused mindset to one that prioritizes quality – of our work, our experiences, and our lives. It's about recognizing that our most valuable contributions often come not from doing more, but from bringing our full presence and creativity to what we do.

By cultivating mindfulness, we can develop the capacity to respond rather than react to workplace demands. This responsiveness allows us to navigate challenges with greater skill and resilience, ultimately leading to more sustainable success and fulfillment in our professional lives.

Consider the potential impact of bringing more awareness and intention to your work day. How might it change your experience of stress? Your ability to focus? Your relationships with colleagues? Your overall sense of fulfillment in your career? These reflections can serve as a starting point for your journey towards becoming a more mindful professional.

As we move into the practical techniques in the following chapters, keep these reflections in mind. The journey to becoming a more mindful professional begins with awareness, and that awareness starts now. Each moment offers an opportunity to step back from the cycle of busyness and choose a more mindful approach to your work and life.

Remember, the goal is not to eliminate busyness entirely – activity and engagement are natural parts of a fulfilling career. Rather, the aim is to bring more consciousness to how we engage with our work, allowing us to navigate the demands of professional life with greater ease, effectiveness, and satisfaction. As we explore the mindfulness techniques in the coming chapters, consider how each might be applied to address the specific challenges you face in your professional life.

CHAPTER 3: MINDFUL BREATHING: YOUR ANCHOR IN THE STORM

In the tumultuous sea of professional life, mindful breathing serves as a steadfast anchor, grounding us in the present moment and providing a refuge from the constant barrage of thoughts, worries, and distractions. This chapter will explore the fundamental importance of breath in mindfulness practice and provide you with practical techniques to harness the power of your breath throughout your workday.

The breath is a unique bodily function in that it operates automatically yet can also be consciously controlled. This duality makes it an ideal focal point for mindfulness practice. By turning our attention to our breath, we create a bridge between the conscious and unconscious aspects of our being, allowing us to influence our physiological state and, by extension, our mental and emotional states.

The science behind mindful breathing is compelling. When we focus on our breath, we activate the parasympathetic nervous system, often referred to as the "rest and digest" system. This counteracts the effects of the sympathetic nervous system, which is responsible for our "fight or flight" response. By consciously engaging in mindful breathing, we can effectively switch our bodies from a state of stress and tension to one of relaxation and calm.

Research has shown that regular practice of mindful breathing can lead to significant physiological changes. Studies have demonstrated that mindful breathing can lower blood pressure, reduce heart rate, and decrease levels of stress hormones like cortisol in the body. These physical changes translate into improved mental and emotional well-being, enhancing our ability to cope with the demands of professional life.

Moreover, mindful breathing has been linked to improved cognitive function. By increasing oxygen flow to the brain and promoting a state of calm alertness, mindful breathing can enhance our ability to concentrate, make decisions, and think creatively. This makes it an invaluable tool for professionals seeking to optimize their mental performance in high-pressure work environments.

In mindfulness practice, the breath serves several crucial functions. Firstly, it acts as a constant, ever-present object of focus. No matter where we are or what we're doing, our breath is always with us, providing a reliable point of return for our wandering attention. Secondly, the rhythm of our breath closely mirrors our mental and emotional states. When we're stressed or anxious, our breathing tends to be shallow and rapid. Conversely, when we're calm and relaxed, our breath is typically deeper and slower. By consciously altering our breath, we can influence our mental and emotional states, creating a sense of calm and balance even in challenging situations.

The breath also serves as a powerful tool for developing present-moment awareness. By focusing on the sensations of breathing – the rise and fall of the chest, the feeling of air moving through the nostrils – we anchor ourselves in the here and now. This can be particularly beneficial in a work environment where we're often pulled between concerns about the future and ruminations about the past.

Furthermore, the practice of mindful breathing can help us develop metacognition – the ability to observe our own thought processes. As we focus on our breath, we inevitably notice when our mind wanders. This noticing is a crucial aspect of mindfulness practice. It helps us become more aware of our thought patterns and mental habits, allowing us to respond to them more skillfully.

Let's begin with a basic mindful breathing exercise that you can practice right at your desk. Start by finding a comfortable seated position, with your feet flat on the floor and your back straight but not rigid. Close your eyes if you feel comfortable doing so, or simply lower your gaze. Now, bring your attention to your breath. Notice the sensation of the air moving in and out of your nostrils, or the rise and fall of your chest or abdomen. Don't try to change your breath in any way; simply observe it as it is.

As you engage in this practice, you may notice various sensations associated with your breath. You might feel the coolness of the air as you inhale and its warmth as you exhale. You might notice the slight pause between each inhale and exhale. Pay attention to these subtle details, allowing them to anchor your awareness in the present moment.

It's important to approach this practice with an attitude of curiosity and non-judgment. There's no "right" or "wrong" way to breathe. Your breath might be shallow or deep, smooth or ragged. Whatever you observe, simply notice it without trying to change or improve it. This acceptance is a key aspect of mindfulness practice.

As you continue to focus on your breath, you may notice that your mind begins to wander. This is entirely normal and expected. When you notice that your attention has drifted, gently guide it back to your breath without judgment. This process of noticing when your mind has wandered and bringing it back to your breath is the essence of mindfulness practice.

It's worth noting that mind-wandering is not a failure of mindfulness practice. In fact, the moment when you notice that your mind has wandered is a moment of mindfulness. It's an opportunity to practice non-judgmental awareness and to consciously redirect your attention. Over time, this process strengthens your ability to focus and increases your overall mindfulness.

Try to maintain this focus on your breath for a few minutes. As you become more comfortable with the practice, you can gradually increase the duration. Even just a few minutes of mindful breathing can have a significant impact on your stress levels and mental clarity.

Now that we've explored a basic mindful breathing exercise, let's look at how you can incorporate breath awareness into your workday. One effective technique is to use transitions between tasks as mindful breathing moments. For example, before you start a new task or enter a meeting, take a few conscious breaths. This brief pause can help you reset your mental state and approach the next activity with greater focus and clarity.

These transitional moments of mindful breathing can serve as a kind of mental "palette cleanser," allowing you to let go of any stress or preoccupations from your previous task and approach the new one with a fresh perspective. They can also help you maintain a sense of continuity and presence throughout your workday, preventing it from becoming a blur of reactive task-switching.

You might consider setting reminders for yourself to take these mindful breathing breaks. This could be a gentle alarm on your phone or computer, or a visual cue in your workspace. The key is to make these moments of mindful breathing a regular part of your work routine, so they become a habit you can rely on throughout your day.

Another approach is to use your breath as a tool for managing stress and anxiety in the moment. When you feel tension rising during a challenging conversation or a stressful presentation, take a moment to focus on your breath. Even a few conscious breaths can help activate your body's relaxation response, reducing stress and allowing you to respond more calmly and effectively to the situation at hand.

This in-the-moment use of mindful breathing can be particularly powerful in high-pressure work situations. By taking a few conscious breaths, you create a pause between the stressful stimulus and your response. This pause allows you to respond more thoughtfully and skillfully, rather than reacting automatically based on stress or anxiety.

It's important to remember that you don't need to make your use of mindful breathing obvious to others. A few subtle, deep breaths can be taken discreetly in almost any work situation. Over time, you may find that this becomes an automatic response to stress, helping you maintain your composure and effectiveness even in challenging circumstances.

For those times when you need a quick reset but don't have the luxury of closing your eyes or taking a break, try this discreet breathing technique: As you inhale, silently count to four. Hold your breath for a count of four, then exhale for a count of four. Repeat this cycle a few times. This simple exercise, known as box breathing, can help regulate your nervous system and bring a sense of calm and focus, even in the midst of a busy workday.

Box breathing, also known as square breathing, is a technique used by everyone from athletes to Navy SEALs to manage stress and improve focus. The equal counts for inhale, hold, exhale, and hold create a rhythm that can quickly bring a sense of calm and balance to your nervous system.

You can adapt this technique to suit your needs and preferences. Some people find a count of four comfortable, while others might prefer a count of five or three. The key is to find a rhythm that feels natural and calming for you. With practice, you may find that even one or two cycles of box breathing can help you reset and refocus.

As you become more comfortable with basic mindful breathing, you may want to explore more advanced techniques for deeper focus. One such technique is the practice of noting. As you focus on your breath, mentally note each inhale and exhale. You might silently say "in" as you inhale and "out" as you exhale. This additional layer of awareness can help anchor your attention more firmly to your breath, reducing mind-wandering and deepening your state of focus.

The practice of noting can be particularly helpful when you're dealing with a lot of mental chatter or distraction. By giving your mind a simple task – noting each breath – you provide it with a focus that can help quiet the stream of thoughts and worries. This can be especially useful in high-stress work situations where you need to maintain your focus and composure.

You can expand on this technique by noting other aspects of your breathing experience. For example, you might note "rising" as your chest or abdomen rises with each inhale, and "falling" as it falls with each exhale. Or you might note the quality of each breath – "deep," "shallow," "smooth," "rough." The key is to keep your noting simple and consistent, using it as a tool to maintain your focus on your breath.

Another advanced technique is to extend your exhales. Start by observing your natural breath for a few cycles. Then, gradually begin to lengthen your exhales, making them slightly longer than your inhales. This extended exhale activates the parasympathetic nervous system, promoting a state of calm and relaxation. This technique can be particularly helpful before important meetings or presentations, or when you need to shift from a state of stress or anxiety to one of calm focus.

The physiological basis for this technique lies in the way our breath interacts with our heart rate. When we inhale, our heart rate slightly increases, and when we exhale, it slightly decreases. By extending our exhales, we prolong this natural deceleration of our heart rate, promoting a greater sense of calm and relaxation.

You might start by making your exhales just slightly longer than your inhales – perhaps inhaling for a count of four and exhaling for a count of five. As you become more comfortable with the technique, you can gradually increase the length of your exhales. Some people find a ratio of 1:2 for inhale to exhale comfortably – for example, inhaling for four counts and exhaling for eight.

It's important to remember that like any skill, mindful breathing takes practice. You may find that your mind wanders frequently at first, or that you forget to practice during busy or stressful times. This is entirely normal. The key is to approach your practice with patience and self-compassion. Each time you remember to take a mindful breath, you're strengthening your capacity for presence and focus.

Consistency is more important than duration when it comes to developing a mindful breathing practice. It's better to take a few mindful breaths several times throughout your day than to have one long session and then forget about it. Try to make mindful breathing a regular part of your work routine – perhaps taking a few mindful breaths at the start of each hour, or before beginning each new task.

It can be helpful to link your mindful breathing practice to specific cues in your work environment. For example, you might take a few mindful breaths each time you sit down at your desk, or when you pick up your phone. By associating your practice with these regular actions, you can build mindful breathing into the fabric of your workday.

As you integrate mindful breathing into your professional life, you may begin to notice subtle but significant changes. You might find that you're better able to maintain your composure during challenging situations, or that you can focus more deeply on complex tasks. You may experience a greater sense of calm and balance throughout your workday, or find that you're less reactive to stress and more responsive to opportunities.

These changes often occur gradually, so it can be helpful to keep a journal of your experiences with mindful breathing. Note any changes you observe in your stress levels, your ability to focus, or your overall sense of well-being at work. This can provide motivation to continue your practice and help you refine your approach over time.

You might also notice changes in your relationships with colleagues. As you become more centered and less reactive, you may find that your interactions become more positive and productive. Your increased calm and presence can have a ripple effect, positively influencing the atmosphere of your workplace.

Remember, the breath is always available to you as an anchor, a tool for self-regulation, and a pathway to greater mindfulness. Whether you're facing a stressful deadline, navigating a difficult conversation, or simply trying to maintain focus during a long workday, your breath is a powerful ally. By cultivating a practice of mindful breathing, you're equipping yourself with a versatile and effective tool for managing the challenges of professional life.

The beauty of mindful breathing is its simplicity and accessibility. You don't need any special equipment or environment to practice – your breath is always with you, ready to be used as a tool for grounding and centering yourself. This makes it an ideal mindfulness technique for busy professionals who may not have the time or opportunity for more formal meditation practices.

As you continue to develop your mindful breathing practice, you may find that it becomes a natural part of your approach to work and life. Rather than being something you do only in response to stress or as a scheduled practice, mindful breathing can become an integral part of how you move through your day, bringing a quality of presence and awareness to all your activities.

As we conclude this chapter, take a moment to reflect on your relationship with your breath. How often do you notice your breath throughout the day? How might increased awareness of your breath impact your work experience? Consider the potential benefits of bringing more conscious breathing into your professional life – not just in terms of stress reduction, but in terms of enhanced focus, improved decision-making, and greater overall well-being.

Set an intention to bring more attention to your breath during your workday. This might be as simple as taking three conscious breaths at the start of each hour, or pausing to connect with your breath before beginning each new task. Remember, every breath is an opportunity to return to the present moment, to reset your mental state, and to approach your work with renewed clarity and purpose.

Your journey to becoming a more mindful professional continues with each conscious breath. As you move forward, remain curious about your experience with mindful breathing. Notice how it affects your stress levels, your ability to focus, and your overall experience of your workday. Be patient with yourself as you develop this practice, knowing that each mindful breath is strengthening your capacity for presence and awareness in your professional life.

CHAPTER 4: MINDFUL BODY AWARENESS: TUNING INTO YOUR PHYSICAL SELF

In the hustle and bustle of professional life, it's easy to become disconnected from our physical selves. We spend hours hunched over keyboards, rushing from meeting to meeting, or sitting through long conference calls, often oblivious to the messages our bodies are sending us. This disconnection can lead to chronic tension, pain, and a host of physical ailments that impact our well-being and productivity. Mindful body awareness offers a powerful antidote to this disconnection, allowing us to tune into our physical selves and cultivate a greater sense of overall well-being.

The modern workplace, with its emphasis on mental tasks and digital interactions, often leads to a neglect of our physical selves. We become so focused on our thoughts, our to-do lists, and our screens that we lose touch with the very vessel that carries us through our day - our body. This disconnection can manifest in various ways: chronic back pain from poor posture, tension headaches from prolonged stress, or even more serious health issues like repetitive strain injuries or cardiovascular problems.

Moreover, this physical disconnection can significantly impact our cognitive performance and emotional well-being. When we're not attuned to our body's signals, we may miss important cues about our stress levels, energy reserves, or need for rest and rejuvenation. This can lead to decreased productivity, increased irritability, and a general sense of being "out of sync" with ourselves and our environment.

The mind-body connection is a fundamental principle in mindfulness practice. Our mental states influence our physical states, and vice versa. When we're stressed, our muscles tense, our breathing becomes shallow, and our heart rate increases. Conversely, when we're relaxed, our muscles loosen, our breathing deepens, and our heart rate slows. By becoming more aware of our physical sensations, we can gain valuable insights into our mental and emotional states, and learn to influence them positively.

This bidirectional relationship between mind and body is supported by a growing body of scientific research. Studies in the field of psychoneuroimmunology have shown that our thoughts and emotions can influence our physical health, affecting everything from our immune system to our cardiovascular health. Conversely, research has demonstrated that physical practices like mindful movement and body awareness can have profound effects on our mental and emotional well-being.

Understanding this mind-body connection can be a powerful tool for professionals seeking to enhance their performance and well-being. By cultivating greater body awareness, we can learn to recognize the early signs of stress or fatigue, allowing us to take proactive steps to maintain our health and productivity. We can also use our body as a resource for grounding ourselves in challenging situations, helping us to stay calm and focused under pressure.

One of the most effective techniques for cultivating body awareness is the body scan meditation. This practice involves systematically bringing attention to different parts of the body, noticing any sensations present without trying to change them. The body scan is a cornerstone practice in many mindfulness-based interventions, including Mindfulness-Based Stress Reduction (MBSR) and Mindfulness-Based Cognitive Therapy (MBCT).

The body scan serves several important functions. First, it helps us develop our capacity for sustained attention, as we practice keeping our focus on physical sensations for an extended period. Second, it enhances our interoceptive awareness - our ability to sense and interpret signals from within our body. This increased interoceptive awareness has been linked to improved emotional regulation and decision-making skills, both of which are crucial in professional settings.

Here's a brief guide to practicing a body scan:

Find a comfortable position, either sitting or lying down. Close your eyes and take a few deep breaths to center yourself. Begin by bringing your attention to your feet. Notice any sensations present - warmth, coolness, tingling, pressure. Don't try to change anything, simply observe. Slowly move your attention up through your body - ankles, calves, knees, thighs, hips, abdomen, chest, back, shoulders, arms, hands, neck, and finally your head. Take your time with each area, spending a few moments to really tune into the sensations present.

As you move through the body scan, you may encounter various types of sensations. You might notice temperature - areas that feel warm or cool. You might become aware of the texture of your clothing against your skin, or the pressure of your body against the chair or floor. You might feel tingling, pulsing, or subtle movements related to your breath or heartbeat. All of these sensations are part of your moment-to-moment physical experience, often overlooked in our busy daily lives.

It's important to approach the body scan with an attitude of curiosity and non-judgment. You're not trying to achieve any particular state or to "fix" anything in your body. Rather, you're simply observing what's already there, developing a deeper awareness of your physical self. This non-judgmental awareness is a key aspect of mindfulness practice and can be particularly valuable in a professional context where we often subject ourselves to harsh self-criticism.

As you practice the body scan, you may notice areas of tension or discomfort that you weren't previously aware of. This awareness is the first step in addressing physical stress and preventing it from accumulating. Regular practice of the body scan can help you become more attuned to your body's signals, allowing you to address tension and discomfort before they become problematic.

This increased awareness can be particularly beneficial in a work context. For example, you might notice that you tend to hold tension in your shoulders when you're under deadline pressure. With this awareness, you can take proactive steps to release this tension - perhaps by doing some gentle shoulder rolls or taking a short break to stretch. Over time, this can help prevent the development of chronic pain or tension-related health issues.

The body scan can also reveal patterns in how we hold stress or emotion in our bodies. You might discover that you clench your jaw when you're frustrated, or that your stomach tightens when you're anxious about a presentation. Recognizing these physical manifestations of our emotional states can provide valuable insights, helping us to manage our stress and emotions more effectively in the workplace.

For busy professionals, finding time for a full body scan meditation may be challenging. However, you can incorporate brief moments of body awareness throughout your workday. For instance, set a reminder on your phone or computer to do a quick body check every hour. Take a moment to notice your posture, any areas of tension, and your overall physical state. This brief check-in can help you make small adjustments that can significantly impact your comfort and well-being over the course of the day.

These mini body awareness breaks can be seamlessly integrated into your work routine. For example, you might do a quick body check while waiting for a meeting to start, or during the transition time between tasks. You could even incorporate a brief body scan into your lunch break, using it as a way to reset and refocus for the afternoon ahead.

As you develop this habit of regular body check-ins, you may find that you become more naturally attuned to your body's signals throughout the day. You might catch yourself slouching and automatically adjust your posture, or notice tension building in your neck and take a moment to stretch. This increased body awareness can lead to improved physical comfort and reduced risk of work-related physical strain or injury.

Desk-friendly stretching exercises are another excellent way to incorporate body awareness into your workday. These exercises not only help to relieve physical tension but also provide an opportunity to tune into your body and break the cycle of sedentary behavior that's common in many office environments. Regular stretching can improve flexibility, reduce muscle tension, and enhance circulation, all of which contribute to better overall health and well-being.

Here's a simple routine you can do right at your desk:

Start with your neck: Gently lower your chin to your chest, feeling the stretch along the back of your neck. Hold for a few breaths, then slowly roll your head to one side, bringing your ear towards your shoulder. Hold, then roll to the other side. As you do this, pay attention to any areas of tightness or resistance. Notice how the stretch feels different on each side of your neck.

Move to your shoulders: Raise your shoulders towards your ears, hold for a moment, then release with an exhale. Repeat a few times. As you lift your shoulders, notice the tension building in the muscles. As you release, focus on the sensation of relaxation spreading through your shoulder and upper back area.

For your arms and wrists: Extend one arm in front of you, palm facing down. Use your other hand to gently pull your fingers back towards your body, feeling the stretch in your forearm. Hold, then switch hands. This stretch can be particularly beneficial for those who spend a lot of time typing or using a mouse. Notice how the stretch extends from your fingers all the way up your forearm.

Finally, for your back: Sit tall in your chair, then gently twist to one side, using the chair arm for support. Hold for a few breaths, feeling the stretch along your spine, then switch sides. As you twist, pay attention to the sensation of your vertebrae rotating and the stretch in the muscles along your spine.

As you perform these stretches, pay close attention to the sensations in your body. Notice where you feel the stretch, any areas of tightness or resistance, and how your body feels as you release each stretch. This mindful approach to stretching not only helps relieve physical tension but also deepens your body awareness.

Remember to breathe deeply and slowly as you stretch. Your breath can serve as an anchor for your attention, helping you stay present with the physical sensations. You might even coordinate your movements with your breath - for example, inhaling as you lift your shoulders, and exhaling as you release them.

It's important to approach these stretches with gentleness and respect for your body's limits. The goal is not to push yourself to the point of pain, but to explore your body's range of motion and to provide relief from the static postures often held during office work. If you have any existing injuries or health conditions, it's advisable to consult with a healthcare professional before starting a new stretching routine.

Mindful walking is another powerful technique for cultivating body awareness. While it may not be feasible to practice formal walking meditation in most work environments, you can bring mindfulness to your everyday movements. As you walk to a meeting or to the break room, pay attention to the sensation of your feet making contact with the ground. Notice the movement of your legs, the swing of your arms, and the rhythm of your breath. This practice not only enhances body awareness but can also serve as a brief mental reset between tasks.

To practice mindful walking, start by slowing down your pace slightly. This doesn't mean you need to walk in slow motion, but just slow enough that you can pay attention to the physical sensations of walking. Notice how your weight shifts from one foot to the other as you walk. Feel the movement of your leg muscles, the bend of your knees, the swing of your arms.

Pay attention to how your foot makes contact with the ground - first the heel, then rolling through to the ball of your foot and toes. Notice the texture of the ground beneath your feet, whether it's carpet, tile, or pavement. As you walk, be aware of the air moving against your skin and the subtle adjustments your body makes to maintain balance.

You can also bring awareness to your posture as you walk. Notice the alignment of your spine, the position of your head, and the set of your shoulders. Are you hunched forward, or is your posture upright and open? How does your posture affect your breathing and overall sense of ease as you move?

Mindful walking can be particularly beneficial when transitioning between different work tasks or environments. For example, you might practice mindful walking as you move from your desk to a meeting room. This can help you arrive at your destination feeling more grounded and present, ready to engage fully in the next task or interaction.

Using body awareness to improve posture is particularly relevant for professionals who spend long hours at a desk. Poor posture can lead to chronic pain and decreased productivity. By regularly checking in with your body, you can catch yourself slumping or hunching and make corrections. Pay attention to the alignment of your spine, the position of your shoulders, and the placement of your feet. Aim for a posture where your ears are aligned with your shoulders, your shoulders are relaxed, and your feet are flat on the floor.

Good posture isn't about rigidly holding yourself in a particular position. Rather, it's about finding a balanced, neutral alignment that allows your body to function optimally. When your posture is aligned, your muscles don't have to work as hard to support your body, reducing fatigue and strain.

To cultivate better posture awareness, try setting up visual cues in your workspace. This might be a sticky note on your computer monitor reminding you to check your posture, or strategically placed objects that prompt you to sit up straight when you see them. You might also consider using ergonomic tools like a standing desk, an ergonomic chair, or a lumbar support cushion to support good posture.

Remember that improving your posture is a gradual process. Your body has likely developed habitual patterns over many years, and it will take time and consistent awareness to create new, healthier patterns. Be patient with yourself and approach posture improvement as an ongoing practice rather than a goal to be achieved.

As you cultivate greater body awareness, you may begin to notice patterns in how your body responds to different work situations. Perhaps your shoulders tense during stressful meetings, or your breathing becomes shallow when you're working on a challenging project. This awareness allows you to implement targeted interventions - a quick shoulder roll, a few deep breaths - to address physical tension as it arises.

These physical patterns can provide valuable insights into your emotional and mental states. For example, you might notice that your jaw clenches when you're feeling frustrated with a colleague, or that your stomach tightens when you're anxious about a deadline. By recognizing these physical manifestations of your emotions, you can gain a deeper understanding of your stress triggers and develop more effective coping strategies.

Moreover, this awareness can help you respond more skillfully to challenging situations. When you notice physical signs of stress or tension arising, you can take proactive steps to address them before they escalate. This might involve taking a short break to stretch or do some deep breathing, or it might mean reassessing your approach to a task that's causing undue stress.

Developing this level of body awareness takes time and practice. You might find it helpful to keep a journal of your physical sensations and the work situations that trigger them. Over time, you'll likely start to see patterns emerge, giving you valuable information about how your body responds to different aspects of your work life.

Remember, the goal of mindful body awareness is not to achieve a state of perfect relaxation or to eliminate all physical discomfort. Rather, it's about developing a more attuned relationship with your body, allowing you to respond to its needs more effectively. This increased awareness can lead to improved physical well-being, reduced stress, and greater overall effectiveness in your professional life.

It's important to approach body awareness practice with an attitude of curiosity and compassion. You may discover areas of chronic tension or discomfort that you've been unconsciously carrying for years. Rather than judging yourself for this, try to view it as useful information that can guide you towards better self-care.

As you become more attuned to your body, you may find that you naturally start making choices that support your physical well-being. This might involve taking more frequent breaks, adjusting your work environment for better ergonomics, or incorporating more movement into your day. These small changes, guided by your increased body awareness, can add up to significant improvements in your overall health and work performance over time.

It's also worth noting that increased body awareness can enhance your presence and effectiveness in professional interactions. When you're more grounded in your physical self, you tend to communicate more clearly and confidently. You're likely to pick up on subtle physical cues from others more easily, enhancing your emotional intelligence and interpersonal skills.

As we conclude this chapter, take a moment to check in with your body. Notice your posture, any areas of tension, and your overall physical state. How might increased body awareness impact your work experience? Consider the potential benefits of bringing more attention to your physical self throughout your workday - not just in terms of comfort and health, but also in terms of your focus, productivity, and interpersonal effectiveness.

Set an intention to incorporate some of the body awareness practices we've discussed into your daily work routine. This might be as simple as doing a quick body scan at the start of each hour, or practicing mindful walking as you move between meetings. Remember, every moment of body awareness is an opportunity to reconnect with yourself and to bring a greater sense of presence and intention to your work.

Your journey towards becoming a more mindful professional continues with each moment of body awareness. As you move forward, remain curious about your physical experiences in the workplace. Notice how different tasks, environments, and interactions affect your body. Use this awareness as a tool for self-care, stress management, and enhanced professional performance.

By cultivating a stronger connection with your physical self, you're laying the foundation for greater overall mindfulness in your professional life. This body awareness will serve as a valuable resource as we continue to explore other aspects of mindfulness in the workplace in the chapters to come.

CHAPTER 5: MINDFUL EATING: NOURISHING BODY AND MIND

In the fast-paced world of modern professionals, eating often becomes a thoughtless act—a hurried sandwich at the desk, a quick snack between meetings, or a late-night binge fueled by stress. We frequently consume our meals while multitasking, barely tasting our food as we rush through emails or prepare for the next presentation. This disconnected approach to eating not only robs us of the pleasure and nourishment that food can provide but also contributes to poor dietary choices, digestive issues, and a disconnection from our body's natural hunger and fullness cues.

The consequences of this mindless eating extend far beyond the immediate moment. Over time, it can lead to a range of health issues, including weight gain, digestive problems, and a dysfunctional relationship with food. In a professional context, these issues can manifest as decreased energy levels, reduced cognitive function, and increased susceptibility to stress-related illnesses. Moreover, the habit of eating while working can blur the boundaries between work and personal time, contributing to burnout and a diminished sense of work-life balance.

Our modern work culture often valorizes constant productivity, making it seem virtuous to work through lunch or snack mindlessly while focusing on tasks. However, this approach is counterproductive. Research has shown that taking proper breaks, including for meals, can actually enhance productivity and creativity. By giving our full attention to our meals, we not only nourish our bodies more effectively but also give our minds a chance to rest and reset, potentially leading to improved performance when we return to our tasks.

Mindful eating offers a powerful antidote to these habits. It's an approach that brings the principles of mindfulness—present-moment awareness and non-judgmental observation—to our relationship with food. By eating mindfully, we can transform our meals from mindless fuel stops into opportunities for nourishment, pleasure, and self-care.

This practice has its roots in ancient Buddhist traditions but has gained significant attention in recent years as a tool for improving both physical and mental health. Mindful eating is not about strict diets or deprivation; rather, it's about developing a more conscious and enjoyable relationship with food. It encourages us to slow down, appreciate our meals, and listen to our body's wisdom about what, when, and how much to eat.

For professionals, mindful eating can serve as a gateway to broader mindfulness practices. The act of eating is something we do multiple times a day, providing frequent opportunities to practice presence and awareness. By cultivating mindfulness around eating, we can develop skills that translate to other areas of our work and life, such as improved focus, better stress management, and enhanced self-awareness.

The principles of mindful eating are simple yet profound. First and foremost, it involves paying full attention to the act of eating. This means engaging all our senses—noticing the colors, smells, textures, and flavors of our food. It also involves eating slowly and deliberately, savoring each bite rather than rushing through our meals.

This sensory engagement serves multiple purposes. On a physical level, it allows our bodies to better register what we're eating, potentially improving digestion and nutrient absorption. On a psychological level, it enhances our enjoyment of food and can lead to greater satisfaction with smaller portions. Furthermore, by fully experiencing our food, we're less likely to seek additional stimulation through overeating or unhealthy food choices.

Eating slowly is a key component of mindful eating that can be particularly challenging for busy professionals accustomed to rushing through meals. However, the benefits are significant. Slower eating allows our bodies time to register fullness, reducing the likelihood of overeating. It also gives us the opportunity to truly taste and appreciate our food, potentially leading to more satisfying meals and healthier food choices over time.

Another key principle is eating without distraction. This means setting aside our work, turning off our screens, and fully focusing on our meal. While this may seem challenging in a busy work environment, even small steps in this direction can make a significant difference.

The habit of eating while working or scrolling through our phones has become deeply ingrained in modern work culture. However, this multitasking approach not only diminishes our enjoyment of food but can also lead to overeating as we're not paying attention to our body's satiety signals. By creating a separation between eating and other activities, we allow ourselves to fully engage with our meal and give our minds a much-needed break from work-related stimuli.

This principle of undistracted eating doesn't mean we can never enjoy a social meal with colleagues or catch up on news during lunch. Rather, it encourages us to be intentional about how we approach our meals. If we choose to combine eating with other activities, we can still strive to bring a quality of awareness to the experience, periodically bringing our attention back to the sensations of eating.

Mindful eating also involves tuning into our body's hunger and fullness cues. Instead of eating by the clock or in response to emotional triggers, we learn to eat when we're hungry and stop when we're satisfied. This can help prevent overeating and promote a healthier relationship with food.

Many of us have lost touch with these natural cues, often ignoring hunger until we're ravenous or eating past the point of comfortable fullness. Mindful eating encourages us to check in with our body regularly, asking ourselves questions like "Am I actually hungry?" or "How full do I feel right now?" Over time, this practice can help us develop a more intuitive approach to eating that better serves our body's needs.

This aspect of mindful eating can be particularly beneficial for professionals who often find their eating patterns dictated by busy schedules rather than genuine hunger. By reconnecting with our body's signals, we can make more informed decisions about when and how much to eat, potentially leading to more stable energy levels throughout the day.

For busy professionals, incorporating mindful eating practices may seem daunting. However, even small moments of mindfulness around food can have a significant impact. Here are some exercises you can try:

The first bite: Before you begin eating, take a moment to look at your food. Notice its colors, textures, and aroma. As you take your first bite, pay full attention to the flavors and sensations in your mouth. This simple practice can help transition your mind from work mode to eating mode.

This "first bite" practice can be particularly powerful as it sets the tone for the rest of the meal. By starting with awareness, we're more likely to maintain some level of mindfulness throughout our eating experience. Even if we can't maintain this level of attention for the entire meal, this initial moment of mindfulness can enhance our overall eating experience.

Mindful sips: If you drink coffee or tea during your workday, use it as an opportunity for mindfulness. As you take a sip, focus entirely on the sensation of the liquid in your mouth, its temperature, and flavor. This can serve as a brief mindfulness break throughout your day.

This practice can be especially beneficial for those who find themselves automatically reaching for their mug without really tasting their beverage. By bringing awareness to these habitual actions, we can transform them into moments of mindfulness that punctuate our workday. Over time, this can help us develop a more general habit of presence and awareness in our professional lives.

Desk-friendly mindful snacking: When you reach for a snack at your desk, pause for a moment. Take three deep breaths before you begin eating. This brief pause can help you assess whether you're eating out of true hunger or in response to stress or boredom.

This pause before snacking can be a powerful tool for breaking unconscious eating habits. It provides a moment to check in with ourselves and our motivations for eating. Are we genuinely hungry, or are we eating to avoid a task, soothe an emotion, or simply out of habit? By bringing awareness to these moments, we can make more conscious choices about our eating habits at work.

Mindful eating can also be a powerful tool for overcoming emotional eating and stress-induced snacking—common challenges for many professionals. By bringing awareness to our eating habits, we can start to recognize the difference between physical hunger and emotional cravings. When you feel the urge to snack, pause and check in with yourself. Are you truly hungry, or are you eating to avoid a task or soothe an uncomfortable emotion?

Emotional eating is often a coping mechanism for dealing with stress, boredom, or difficult emotions. In a professional context, we might find ourselves reaching for snacks when we're procrastinating on a challenging task, feeling anxious about a presentation, or dealing with conflict with a colleague. By bringing mindfulness to these moments, we can start to identify the underlying emotional triggers for our eating habits.

This awareness is the first step in developing healthier coping mechanisms. Once we recognize that we're eating in response to emotions rather than physical hunger, we can explore alternative ways to address these feelings. This might involve taking a short break, practicing some deep breathing, or finding a more constructive way to address the underlying issue.

If you identify that you're eating for emotional reasons, try this exercise: Instead of immediately reaching for food, take a few deep breaths. Notice any emotions or physical sensations present. Ask yourself what you truly need in this moment. Sometimes, a short walk, a stretch, or a few minutes of deep breathing can address the underlying need more effectively than food.

This pause and check-in can be a powerful tool for breaking the automatic cycle of emotional eating. By creating a space between the trigger (emotion) and the response (eating), we give ourselves the opportunity to make a more conscious choice. This doesn't mean we should never eat for comfort or pleasure, but rather that we should do so with awareness and intention.

It's also worth noting that sometimes, what we perceive as hunger might actually be thirst, fatigue, or a need for a break from work. By pausing to check in with ourselves, we can better identify what our body and mind truly need in that moment. This can lead to more effective self-care practices that go beyond just eating.

Mindful meal planning and preparation can also contribute significantly to healthier eating habits. Take some time at the beginning of each week to plan your meals. As you plan, consider not just nutrition but also what foods you truly enjoy and find satisfying. When you prepare your meals, engage fully in the process. Notice the colors and textures of the ingredients, the sounds and smells of cooking. This mindful approach to meal preparation can make the act of cooking a form of stress relief rather than an additional chore.

For busy professionals, meal planning can be a game-changer. It not only ensures that we have healthy options readily available, reducing the likelihood of resorting to fast food or vending machine snacks, but it also eliminates the daily stress of deciding what to eat. By approaching meal planning mindfully, we can create a balance between nutrition, convenience, and enjoyment.

Mindful meal preparation can also serve as a form of active meditation. The repetitive actions of chopping vegetables or stirring a pot can be grounding and calming. By fully engaging with these processes, we can create a mental break from work-related thoughts and potentially return to our tasks with renewed focus and creativity.

For those who don't enjoy cooking or have limited time, mindful meal preparation can still be incorporated into simpler food choices. Even if you're just assembling a sandwich or salad, you can do so with full attention, appreciating the colors, textures, and aromas of the ingredients. This approach can transform even the simplest meal into a more satisfying and mindful experience.

Creating a mindful eating environment at work can be challenging but is not impossible. If you have the option, try to step away from your desk for meals. Even if it's just for 15 minutes, eating in a different environment can help you focus more fully on your meal. If you must eat at your desk, try to create a small ritual that separates your mealtime from work time. This could be as simple as clearing a space on your desk, using real cutlery instead of plastic, or taking a moment to arrange your food attractively.

The physical environment in which we eat can significantly impact our eating experience. Eating at our desk, surrounded by work-related items and potential stressors, can make it difficult to fully disconnect and enjoy our meal. By creating a dedicated eating space, even if it's just a cleared corner of our desk, we signal to our mind that it's time to shift focus from work to nourishment.

If your workplace has a break room or outdoor area, consider using these spaces for your meals. The change of scenery can provide a mental break from work and make it easier to focus on your food. If you're working from home, try to eat in a different room from where you work, or at least move to a different part of your workspace for meals.

The idea of creating a ritual around mealtime can be particularly powerful. This doesn't have to be elaborate – it could be as simple as taking a moment to arrange your food nicely on your plate, or taking three deep breaths before you begin eating. These small actions can help signal to your brain that it's time to switch gears from work mode to eating mode.

As you incorporate these mindful eating practices into your work life, you may begin to notice changes. You might find that you enjoy your food more, even if it's the same lunch you've had many times before. You may notice that you feel more satisfied with smaller portions, or that you're better able to resist the lure of unhealthy snacks. You might even find that these moments of mindfulness around food serve as welcome breaks in your day, helping you return to your work with renewed focus and energy.

These changes often occur gradually, so it can be helpful to keep a journal of your experiences with mindful eating. Note any shifts you observe in your eating habits, energy levels, or overall well-being. This can provide motivation to continue your practice and help you identify which strategies are most effective for you.

You might also notice improvements in your digestion. When we eat mindfully, we tend to chew our food more thoroughly and eat more slowly, which can aid in digestion. Additionally, by reducing stress around mealtimes, we support our body's natural digestive processes.

Another benefit you might experience is a reduction in work-related stress. By using mealtimes as opportunities for mindfulness, you create natural breaks in your workday where you can reset and recharge. This can lead to improved focus and productivity when you return to your tasks.

Remember, like all mindfulness practices, mindful eating is a skill that develops over time. Be patient with yourself as you explore these techniques. Some days, you may find it easy to eat mindfully; other days, you may fall back into old habits. The key is to approach each meal with fresh intention, without judgment for past choices.

It's important to recognize that perfectionism around mindful eating can be counterproductive. The goal is not to eat mindfully 100% of the time, but rather to bring more awareness to our eating habits overall. Even small moments of mindfulness around food can have a significant impact on our relationship with eating and our overall well-being.

As you continue to practice mindful eating, you may find that its principles start to extend beyond mealtimes. The awareness and presence you cultivate during eating can begin to infuse other areas of your work life. You might find yourself approaching tasks with greater focus, or navigating workplace relationships with more intention and clarity.

Mindful eating can also serve as a gateway to exploring other mindfulness practices. As you become more comfortable with bringing awareness to your eating habits, you might feel inspired to explore meditation, mindful movement, or other mindfulness techniques that can further enhance your professional and personal life.

As we conclude this chapter, consider setting an intention around mindful eating for your next workday. Perhaps you'll commit to eating lunch away from your desk, or to taking three mindful bites at the start of each meal. Whatever you choose, approach it with curiosity and openness. Your journey towards becoming a more mindful professional extends to every aspect of your day, including the vital act of nourishing your body and mind through mindful eating.

Remember that mindful eating is not about adhering to strict rules or achieving a perfect state of awareness. It's about cultivating a more conscious and enjoyable relationship with food. As you integrate these practices into your work life, be kind to yourself and celebrate even small moments of mindfulness around eating.

Consider sharing your experiences with colleagues or starting a mindful eating group at work. This can provide support and accountability as you develop your practice, and might even inspire positive changes in your workplace's food culture.

Ultimately, mindful eating is about more than just food – it's about bringing greater awareness, intention, and joy to an essential part of our daily lives. By nourishing ourselves mindfully, we enhance our overall well-being and equip ourselves to meet the challenges of our professional lives with greater resilience and clarity.

CHAPTER 6: MINDFUL COMMUNICATION: ENHANCING PROFESSIONAL RELATIONSHIPS

In the complex web of professional life, effective communication stands as a cornerstone of success. Yet, in our rush to convey information, meet deadlines, and achieve goals, we often lose sight of the deeper aspects of communication. Mindful communication offers a path to more meaningful, effective, and satisfying interactions in the workplace, enhancing our professional relationships and overall effectiveness.

The importance of communication in professional settings cannot be overstated. It forms the basis of teamwork, leadership, negotiation, and virtually every aspect of organizational function. However, the quality of our communication often suffers in the face of workplace pressures, time constraints, and the sheer volume of information we need to process and convey on a daily basis.

Mindful communication provides a framework for elevating

the quality of our professional interactions. It encourages us to bring full presence and awareness to our communications, fostering deeper understanding, stronger relationships, and more productive collaborations. By applying mindfulness principles to how we speak, listen, and interact, we can transform our professional communication from a routine task into a powerful tool for connection and effectiveness.

At the heart of mindful communication lies the practice of active listening. This goes beyond simply hearing the words someone is saying; it involves fully engaging with the speaker, seeking to understand not just their words, but their intentions, emotions, and underlying messages. Active listening requires us to set aside our own agenda, resist the urge to formulate our response while the other person is speaking, and instead give our full attention to what is being communicated.

Active listening is a skill that can dramatically improve our professional relationships and effectiveness. When we truly listen to our colleagues, we gain deeper insights into their perspectives, concerns, and ideas. This not only helps us understand and address issues more effectively but also fosters an environment of respect and collaboration.

Moreover, active listening can help us pick up on subtle cues and nuances that we might otherwise miss. In a professional context, these subtle elements of communication can often be crucial to understanding the full picture of a situation or identifying potential issues before they become problems.

To practice active listening, start by giving the speaker your undivided attention. Put away your phone, turn away from your computer screen, and face the speaker directly. As they speak, observe not just their words, but their tone of voice, facial expressions, and body language. These non-verbal cues often convey as much, if not more, than the words themselves.

This level of attention can be challenging in a world full of distractions, but it's a skill that can be developed with practice. Start by committing to giving your full attention in short bursts

– perhaps for the first five minutes of a conversation or meeting. As you become more comfortable with this level of focus, you can gradually extend the duration of your active listening practice.

Pay attention to your own internal responses as you listen. Notice any urges to interrupt, disagree, or offer your own perspective. Rather than acting on these impulses, simply observe them and return your focus to the speaker. This practice of noticing and redirecting your attention is at the core of mindfulness and can greatly enhance your ability to listen effectively.

While listening, resist the urge to interrupt or offer solutions immediately. Instead, use small verbal and non-verbal cues to show you're engaged – a nod, an "mm-hmm," or a brief "I see." When the speaker has finished, try paraphrasing what you've heard to ensure you've understood correctly. This not only helps clarify any misunderstandings but also demonstrates to the speaker that you've been truly listening.

Paraphrasing is a powerful tool in active listening. It involves restating the speaker's message in your own words, which serves several purposes. First, it allows you to check your understanding of what's been said. Second, it shows the speaker that you've been paying attention and are making an effort to understand their perspective. Finally, it gives the speaker an opportunity to clarify or expand on any points that you might have misunderstood.

When paraphrasing, be sure to focus on the key points and overall message, rather than trying to repeat everything verbatim. Use phrases like "So what I'm hearing is..." or "It sounds like you're saying..." to introduce your paraphrase. This technique can be particularly useful in complex or emotionally charged conversations, where ensuring mutual understanding is crucial.

Mindful speaking is the natural counterpart to active listening. It involves choosing our words with intention, being aware of the impact of our communication, and speaking from a place of authenticity and respect. Before speaking, especially in important or potentially challenging conversations, take a moment to check in with yourself. What is your intention in this communication?

Are you seeking to inform, persuade, connect, or something else? Being clear about your intention can help guide your choice of words and tone.

This practice of pausing before speaking can be transformative in our professional communications. In the heat of a discussion or the pressure of a meeting, we often speak reactively, without fully considering our words or their impact. By taking even a brief moment to check in with ourselves, we can shift from reactive to responsive communication.

Consider the difference between reacting and responding. A reaction is often automatic, driven by our immediate emotions or impulses. A response, on the other hand, is thoughtful and intentional. By practicing mindful speaking, we cultivate the ability to respond rather than react in our professional interactions.

As you speak, pay attention to your pace and tone. Are you rushing through your words, or speaking calmly and clearly? Is your tone conveying the emotion you intend? Be aware of any tendencies you might have to use filler words or hedge your statements, as these can undermine the clarity and confidence of your communication.

The pace of our speech can have a significant impact on how our message is received. Speaking too quickly can make us seem nervous or unprepared, while speaking too slowly might cause our listeners to lose interest. Aim for a pace that feels natural and allows your listeners to easily follow your train of thought.

Tone of voice is another crucial element of mindful speaking. Our tone can convey emotions and attitudes that may not be explicitly stated in our words. In professional settings, it's important to ensure that our tone aligns with our intended message and is appropriate for the context. This doesn't mean we need to be emotionless or overly formal, but rather that we should be intentional about the emotional content we're conveying through our tone.

Non-verbal communication awareness is another crucial aspect of mindful communication. Our body language, facial expressions, and even our physical presence in a space all communicate messages, often unconsciously. Take time to become aware of your habitual non-verbal communication patterns. Do you tend to cross your arms when feeling defensive? Do you make eye contact when speaking, or do you avoid it? By becoming more aware of these patterns, you can begin to align your non-verbal communication with your intended message more effectively.

Body language is a powerful form of communication that can either reinforce or contradict our verbal messages. In professional settings, being aware of and intentional about our body language can significantly enhance our effectiveness as communicators. For example, maintaining an open posture (uncrossed arms, relaxed shoulders) can help convey openness and receptivity, while making appropriate eye contact can demonstrate engagement and confidence.

It's also important to be aware of cultural differences in non-verbal communication. What's considered appropriate eye contact or personal space can vary significantly across cultures. In diverse professional environments, being mindful of these differences can help prevent misunderstandings and foster more inclusive communication.

Facial expressions are another key component of non-verbal communication. Our faces often betray our true feelings, even when we're trying to maintain a neutral expression. By bringing awareness to our facial expressions, we can ensure that they align with our intended message and the professional context. This doesn't mean we need to maintain a constant smile or suppress all emotional expression, but rather that we should be conscious of what our face is communicating.

In today's digital age, a significant portion of our professional communication happens through emails, instant messages, and other digital platforms. Mindfulness in digital communication is perhaps even more crucial, as these mediums lack the nuance of face-to-face interaction. Before sending an email or message, take a moment to re-read it. Consider not just the content, but the tone. How might the recipient interpret your words? Are you conveying the intended message clearly and respectfully?

Digital communication presents unique challenges and opportunities for mindful communication. On one hand, the asynchronous nature of many digital communications allows us more time to craft our messages thoughtfully. On the other hand, the lack of non-verbal cues and immediate feedback can lead to misunderstandings or misinterpretations.

When composing digital communications, be particularly mindful of your word choice and sentence structure. Without the context provided by tone of voice and body language, your words carry even more weight. Consider using emojis or other digital cues judiciously to help convey tone in appropriate contexts.

When composing digital communications, be aware of the tendency to react quickly, especially to messages that provoke an emotional response. If you receive a challenging email or message, take a few deep breaths before responding. Consider whether an immediate response is necessary, or if taking some time to reflect would lead to a more thoughtful and effective communication.

The immediacy of digital communication can often lead us to respond reactively, especially to messages that trigger strong emotions. However, in professional settings, these quick reactions can often lead to regret or escalated conflicts. By practicing mindfulness in our digital communications, we can create a buffer between the trigger (the message we receive) and our response.

If you find yourself feeling emotionally charged after receiving a digital communication, try this mindfulness practice: Close your eyes and take three deep breaths. Notice any physical sensations or emotions present. Then, ask yourself: "What's the most skillful way to respond to this message?" This brief pause can help you shift from a reactive to a responsive mode of communication.

Handling difficult conversations with mindfulness is perhaps one of the most valuable skills we can develop as professionals.

Whether it's giving critical feedback, addressing a conflict, or negotiating a challenging situation, approaching these conversations mindfully can lead to more positive outcomes.

Difficult conversations are an inevitable part of professional life, but they're often the conversations we're least prepared for. We might avoid them out of fear of conflict, rush through them to get them over with, or approach them with a combative attitude. Mindfulness offers a different approach – one that allows us to navigate these challenging interactions with greater skill and compassion.

One key aspect of mindful difficult conversations is maintaining awareness of our own emotional state. It's natural for challenging conversations to trigger stress responses or defensive reactions. By staying tuned in to our own internal experience, we can notice when we're becoming triggered and take steps to regain our composure.

Before entering a difficult conversation, take some time to center yourself. A few minutes of mindful breathing can help calm your nervous system and bring you into a more balanced state. Set an intention for the conversation – perhaps to listen openly, to speak truthfully but kindly, or to work towards a mutually beneficial solution.

Setting an intention for a difficult conversation can be a powerful practice. It helps orient our mind towards a positive outcome and reminds us of our higher purpose in the interaction. Your intention might be something like "To understand the other person's perspective fully" or "To communicate my concerns clearly and respectfully."

It can also be helpful to visualize a positive outcome for the conversation. Spend a few moments imagining the conversation going well, with both parties feeling heard and respected. This positive visualization can help reduce anxiety and prime you for a more constructive interaction.

During the conversation, stay present. Notice if you're becoming defensive or if your mind is racing ahead to formulate arguments. If you feel yourself becoming reactive, take a breath and reconnect with your intention. Remember to listen actively, seeking to understand the other person's perspective fully before responding.

Staying present during difficult conversations can be challenging, as our mind often wants to race ahead to plan our response or replay past interactions. One technique for staying present is to periodically check in with your physical sensations. Notice the feeling of your feet on the ground, or the sensation of your breath moving in and out. These physical anchors can help bring you back to the present moment when your mind starts to wander.

Another key aspect of mindful difficult conversations is cultivating empathy. Try to put yourself in the other person's shoes, even if you disagree with their perspective. What might be driving their behavior or viewpoint? This empathetic stance can help de-escalate tensions and open up possibilities for mutual understanding.

After the conversation, take some time to reflect. What went well? What could you have done differently? Use these reflections to continually refine your communication skills. This post-conversation reflection is a crucial part of the learning process. It allows us to integrate the lessons from each interaction and apply them to future conversations.

Consider keeping a communication journal where you record your reflections on important or challenging conversations. Over time, this can help you identify patterns in your communication style and track your progress as you develop your mindful communication skills.

As you incorporate these mindful communication practices into your professional life, you may begin to notice shifts in your relationships and interactions. You might find that your colleagues open up to you more, that misunderstandings occur less frequently, or that you're able to navigate challenging situations with greater ease.

These changes often occur gradually, so be patient with yourself and others as you develop your mindful communication skills. You might start to notice small shifts – perhaps you catch yourself before interrupting in a meeting, or you're able to listen more attentively to a colleague's concerns.

Over time, these small shifts can lead to significant improvements in your professional relationships and overall work environment. Colleagues may come to see you as a trusted listener and effective communicator. You might find that your team's collaboration improves as mindful communication practices spread.

Remember, like all aspects of mindfulness, communication is a practice. There will be times when you fall short of your intentions, when you react without thinking, or when you fail to listen as attentively as you'd like. The key is to approach each interaction as a fresh opportunity to practice mindful communication, learning and growing with each experience.

When you do slip up – perhaps speaking harshly in a moment of stress or failing to listen attentively – treat it as an opportunity for learning rather than a failure. Reflect on what led to the lapse in mindful communication and how you might handle a similar situation differently in the future. If appropriate, don't hesitate to apologize and recommit to your intention of communicating mindfully.

It can also be helpful to find a "mindful communication buddy" at work – someone who shares your interest in developing these skills. You can check in with each other regularly, share experiences and challenges, and offer support in your respective practices.

As we conclude this chapter, consider setting an intention for your next professional interaction. Perhaps you'll focus on listening more attentively in your next meeting, or on bringing more awareness to your non-verbal communication. Whatever you choose, approach it with curiosity and openness.

Remember that mindful communication is not about perfection, but about presence and intention. Each interaction is an opportunity to practice, learn, and grow. As you continue to develop your mindful communication skills, you'll likely find that not only do your professional relationships improve, but your overall experience of work becomes more satisfying and meaningful.

Your journey towards becoming a more mindful professional continues with each mindful word spoken and each moment of attentive listening. As you move forward, remain curious about your communication experiences. Notice how different approaches affect your interactions and relationships. And above all, be kind to yourself as you develop these crucial skills. The path of mindful communication is a lifelong journey, one that can profoundly enrich both your professional and personal life.

CHAPTER 7: MINDFUL TIME MANAGEMENT: DOING MORE BY DOING LESS

In the realm of professional life, time is often viewed as our most precious and scarce resource. We find ourselves constantly racing against the clock, trying to squeeze more tasks into each day, often at the expense of our well-being and the quality of our work. The conventional approach to time management often revolves around multitasking and maximizing every minute. However, mindful time management offers a different perspective – one that focuses on the quality of our attention and the intentionality of our actions.

This shift in perspective is crucial in today's fast-paced work environment. The pressure to be constantly productive, to always be "on," has led to a culture of chronic stress and burnout. We've been conditioned to equate busyness with productivity and worth, often at the cost of our mental health and the quality of our output. Mindful time management challenges this paradigm, encouraging us to slow down, focus, and make deliberate choices about how we spend our time.

The concept of mindful time management is rooted in the broader principles of mindfulness – being fully present in the moment, aware of our thoughts and actions without judgment. When applied to how we manage our time, these principles can transform our work experience, leading to greater efficiency, creativity, and satisfaction.

The myth of multitasking is perhaps one of the most pervasive misconceptions in modern work culture. We pride ourselves on our ability to juggle multiple tasks simultaneously, believing that this increases our productivity. However, numerous studies have shown that what we perceive as multitasking is actually rapid task-switching, which can reduce productivity by as much as 40%. Each time we switch tasks, our brain needs time to refocus, leading to a phenomenon known as "attention residue." This residual attention from the previous task interferes with our performance on the new task, reducing our efficiency and increasing the likelihood of errors.

The cognitive cost of multitasking is significant. When we constantly switch between tasks, we're not giving our brain the opportunity to fully engage with any single task. This not only impacts the quality of our work but also increases mental fatigue. We might feel like we're being productive because we're busy, but in reality, we're working less efficiently and effectively than if we focused on one task at a time.

Moreover, the habit of multitasking can have long-term effects on our ability to concentrate. Some studies suggest that chronic multitasking can lead to decreased gray matter density in brain regions associated with cognitive control and emotional regulation. In essence, by trying to do everything at once, we may be diminishing our capacity to focus deeply on anything.

Instead of multitasking, mindful time management embraces the principle of single-tasking or monotasking. This involves giving our full attention to one task at a time, completing it (or reaching a natural stopping point) before moving on to the next. Single-tasking allows us to engage more deeply with our work, leading to higher quality output and a greater sense of accomplishment.

The practice of single-tasking aligns closely with the concept of "flow" in psychology – a state of complete absorption in an activity, where we lose track of time and self-consciousness. By focusing on one task at a time, we're more likely to enter this highly productive and satisfying state of flow.

Single-tasking also helps reduce the mental clutter and anxiety that often accompanies multitasking. When we're trying to juggle multiple tasks, there's always a nagging feeling that we're forgetting something or falling behind. By focusing on one task at a time, we can give our full attention to the present moment, reducing stress and increasing our sense of control over our work.

To practice single-tasking, start by identifying the most important task for your day. Block out a specific time for this task and commit to working on it without interruption. Close unnecessary browser tabs, put your phone on silent, and if possible, find a quiet space where you won't be disturbed. As you work, if you notice your mind wandering to other tasks or concerns, gently bring your attention back to the task at hand. This is the essence of mindfulness in action – noticing when our attention has drifted and bringing it back without judgment.

It's important to note that transitioning to single-tasking can be challenging, especially if you're used to a multitasking work style. You might feel restless or anxious at first, with a strong urge to check your email or switch to another task. This is normal. Treat these moments as opportunities to practice mindfulness – notice the urge without acting on it, and gently redirect your attention back to the task at hand.

Start small when incorporating single-tasking into your work routine. You might begin with 15-minute focused work sessions, gradually increasing the duration as you build your concentration muscle. Remember, the goal is not to maintain perfect focus for hours on end, but to cultivate a habit of giving your full attention to one task at a time.

Closely related to single-tasking is the concept of deep work, popularized by author Cal Newport. Deep work refers to the ability to focus without distraction on a cognitively demanding task. It's in these states of deep focus that we produce our most valuable and creative work. However, in our constantly connected work environments, opportunities for deep work are becoming increasingly rare.

The concept of deep work challenges the notion that being constantly available and responsive is the key to professional success. While quick responses and frequent communication have their place, it's the ability to dive deep into complex problems and produce high-quality work that often sets exceptional professionals apart.

Deep work is not just about productivity – it's about fulfillment. When we engage in deep work, we're more likely to experience a sense of accomplishment and satisfaction with our work. This can lead to greater job satisfaction and a stronger sense of professional identity.

To incorporate more deep work into your schedule, try blocking out specific times for focused work. During these periods, eliminate all distractions and commit to working on a single, important task. You might start with 30-minute blocks and gradually increase the duration as your capacity for sustained focus improves. Remember, like any skill, the ability to engage in deep work improves with practice.

Creating an environment conducive to deep work is crucial. This might involve finding a quiet space, using noise-canceling headphones, or using apps that block distracting websites. Some professionals find it helpful to create a specific ritual that signals the start of a deep work session – this could be as simple as brewing a cup of tea or setting up your workspace in a particular way.

It's also important to communicate your deep work schedule to colleagues. Let them know when you'll be unavailable for quick questions or chats, and when you'll be back online. This sets clear expectations and helps protect your focused work time.

Using mindfulness to prioritize tasks is another crucial aspect of effective time management. Often, we react to our to-do lists, tackling whatever seems most urgent or whatever has been requested most recently. However, this reactive approach can lead us to spend time on tasks that aren't truly important or aligned with our goals.

Mindful prioritization involves taking a step back and considering our tasks in the context of our broader goals and values. It's about making conscious choices about where to invest our time and energy, rather than simply reacting to the loudest demands.

To prioritize mindfully, take a few moments at the start of each day (or the end of the previous day) to review your tasks. Take a few deep breaths to center yourself, then look at each task on your list. Ask yourself: Is this truly important? Does it align with my goals and values? What impact will completing this task have? This mindful reflection can help you identify the tasks that deserve your time and energy, allowing you to focus on what truly matters.

Consider using a prioritization matrix, such as the Eisenhower Box, to categorize your tasks based on their importance and urgency. This can help you visually separate tasks that are truly important from those that just feel urgent. Remember, not everything that's urgent is important, and not everything that's important is urgent.

As you prioritize, be mindful of your energy levels and natural rhythms. Align your most important and challenging tasks with the times when you're typically most alert and focused. This might mean tackling your most crucial work first thing in the morning, or it might mean scheduling important tasks for after lunch if that's when you tend to have a surge of energy.

Mindful scheduling and calendar management involve being intentional about how we allocate our time. Instead of simply reacting to meeting invites and deadlines, take a proactive approach to shaping your schedule. Block out time for important tasks, including periods for deep work. Schedule breaks and transitions between tasks – these moments of pause can help you reset and approach each new task with fresh energy.

When scheduling, be realistic about how long tasks will take. We often underestimate the time required for complex tasks, leading to overcommitment and stress. Build in buffer time between tasks to allow for unexpected delays or to give yourself a moment to breathe and reset.

Be mindful of your natural energy rhythms when scheduling. If you're most alert and focused in the morning, schedule your most challenging or important tasks during this time. Reserve lower-energy periods for more routine tasks or administrative work.

Consider the concept of "time blocking" – assigning specific blocks of time to certain types of tasks or projects. This can help create a sense of structure and rhythm to your day, while also ensuring that you're allocating sufficient time to your most important work.

The Pomodoro Technique is a time management method that aligns well with mindfulness principles. It involves working in focused 25-minute intervals (called "Pomodoros"), followed by short breaks. This technique helps maintain focus while also preventing burnout. During each Pomodoro, commit to working on a single task without interruption. Use the breaks as opportunities to practice brief mindfulness exercises – a few mindful breaths, a quick body scan, or simply looking away from your screen and focusing on a distant object to rest your eyes.

The Pomodoro Technique can be particularly effective for tasks that you find challenging or that you tend to procrastinate on. The time-limited nature of each work session can make intimidating tasks feel more manageable, while the regular breaks help prevent mental fatigue.

During your Pomodoro breaks, resist the urge to check email or engage in other work-related tasks. These breaks are an opportunity to truly rest and reset your mind. Stand up, stretch, get a glass of water, or simply close your eyes and take a few deep breaths. These moments of pause are crucial for maintaining focus and preventing burnout over the course of your workday.

As you implement these mindful time management practices, you may find that you're actually doing less – fewer tasks, fewer distractions, fewer context switches. However, you're likely to find that the quality and impact of your work improves. You may experience a greater sense of accomplishment and satisfaction with your work, as well as reduced stress and overwhelm.

This shift from quantity to quality is at the heart of mindful time management. By focusing on fewer tasks but giving them our full attention, we often produce better results in less time. This approach allows us to work smarter, not just harder.

You might also notice improvements in your ability to focus and in your overall sense of calm throughout the workday. By reducing the mental clutter that comes with constant task-switching and reacting to every notification, you create space for clearer thinking and more intentional action.

Remember, mindful time management is not about rigid control or perfect productivity. It's about bringing awareness and intentionality to how we use our time. There will be days when things don't go as planned, when interruptions are unavoidable, or when you struggle to focus. The key is to approach each moment, each task, with fresh awareness and without judgment.

When things don't go according to plan, treat it as an opportunity to practice flexibility and self-compassion. Instead of getting frustrated or giving up on your mindful approach, simply notice what happened and gently redirect yourself back to your intentions.

It's also important to remember that mindful time management extends beyond work hours. Consider how you transition between work and personal time, especially if you work from home. Create rituals that signal the end of your workday, allowing you to fully disconnect and recharge.

As we conclude this chapter, take a moment to reflect on your current approach to time management. How might incorporating these mindful practices shift your relationship with time and productivity? Consider the potential benefits not just in terms of work output, but also in terms of your overall well-being and job satisfaction.

Consider choosing one technique – perhaps single-tasking or mindful prioritization – to focus on in the coming week. Start small and be patient with yourself as you develop these new habits. Remember, the goal is progress, not perfection.

Your journey towards becoming a more mindful professional continues with each intentional moment and each mindful choice about how you invest your time and attention. As you move forward, remain curious about your experience. Notice how different approaches affect your productivity, your stress levels, and your overall satisfaction with your work.

By bringing mindfulness to how we manage our time, we can transform our experience of work from one of constant pressure and overwhelm to one of purposeful engagement and fulfillment. This shift not only benefits us as individuals but can also contribute to a more positive and productive work environment for our colleagues and organizations as a whole.

CHAPTER 8: MINDFUL DECISION MAKING: CLARITY IN THE FACE OF COMPLEXITY

In the fast-paced world of modern business, professionals are called upon to make countless decisions each day. From minor choices about how to prioritize tasks to major strategic decisions that can impact the entire organization, our ability to make sound judgments is constantly put to the test. The complexity of these decisions, coupled with the pressure to act quickly, can often lead to stress, overwhelm, and less-than-optimal outcomes. This is where mindful decision making comes into play, offering a pathway to greater clarity, confidence, and effectiveness in our professional choices.

The sheer volume of decisions we face in our professional lives can be staggering. Research suggests that the average adult makes about 35,000 remotely conscious decisions each day. In a work context, many of these decisions carry significant weight, impacting not just our own work but often the work of our colleagues and the success of our organizations. This constant demand for decision making can lead to a state of cognitive overload, where our ability to think clearly and make wise choices becomes compromised.

Moreover, the modern work environment often emphasizes speed over thoughtfulness. We're expected to make quick decisions, to be agile and responsive in the face of rapidly changing circumstances. While there's certainly value in being able to think on our feet, this pressure for rapid decision making can lead to hasty choices that we later regret. Mindful decision making offers a way to balance the need for timeliness with the importance of thoughtful consideration.

The impact of mindfulness on cognitive function is well-documented in scientific literature. Regular mindfulness practice has been shown to enhance areas of the brain associated with decision making, including the prefrontal cortex, which is responsible for executive functions such as planning, problem-solving, and emotional regulation. By cultivating mindfulness, we can literally reshape our brains to become better decision-makers. Neuroscientific research has revealed that mindfulness meditation can increase the thickness of the prefrontal cortex and enhance connectivity between different brain regions. This improved neural integration allows for more holistic decision making, where we're able to consider multiple perspectives and potential outcomes more effectively. In essence, mindfulness practice equips our brains with better hardware for decision making.

Furthermore, mindfulness has been shown to reduce activity in the amygdala, the brain's fear center. This reduction in amygdala activity can help us approach decisions with less emotional reactivity and more rational consideration. When we're less driven by fear or anxiety, we're better able to assess situations clearly and make choices aligned with our long-term goals and values.

One of the key benefits of mindful decision making is its ability to help us overcome decision fatigue. Decision fatigue refers to the deteriorating quality of decisions made after a long session of decision making. As we make decision after decision throughout our workday, our ability to make good choices becomes depleted, often leading to either rash decisions or decision paralysis.

Decision fatigue is a well-documented phenomenon in psychology. Studies have shown that judges are more likely to give unfavorable rulings later in the day, and consumers are more likely to make impulsive purchases after a long shopping trip. In a professional context, decision fatigue can lead to poor choices in important matters simply because they come at the end of a long day of decision making.

Recognizing the signs of decision fatigue is crucial. These might include feeling overwhelmed by choices, procrastinating on important decisions, making impulsive choices, or avoiding decision making altogether. By being aware of these signs, we can take steps to mitigate the effects of decision fatigue and approach important choices with a fresher mind.

To combat decision fatigue, try incorporating brief mindfulness practices throughout your day. For example, before making an important decision, take a few moments to practice mindful breathing. Close your eyes, take several deep breaths, and bring your attention fully to the present moment. This short pause can help reset your mind, reducing the cumulative effects of decision fatigue and allowing you to approach the choice with fresh perspective.

These mindful pauses serve multiple purposes. First, they give our brains a brief rest from the constant demands of decision making. Second, they help bring us back to the present moment, grounding us in current reality rather than getting lost in projections about potential outcomes. Finally, they create a space between stimulus and response, allowing us to choose our reaction rather than responding automatically.

In addition to mindful breathing, other quick mindfulness practices can be effective in combating decision fatigue. These might include a brief body scan, a moment of gratitude reflection, or even a short walk with attention to your surroundings. The key is to find practices that work for you and can be easily integrated into your workday.

Mindful reflection techniques can significantly enhance our decision-making process. One such technique is the STOP method: Stop, Take a breath, Observe, Proceed. When faced with a decision, especially one that feels urgent or emotionally charged, pause and apply this method. Stop whatever you're doing, Take a breath to center yourself, Observe your thoughts, emotions, and the facts of the situation without judgment, then Proceed with your decision. This brief intervention can prevent reactive decision making and allow for a more thoughtful, intentional approach.

The STOP method is particularly useful in high-pressure situations where we might be tempted to react impulsively. By creating a deliberate pause, we give ourselves the opportunity to step back from the immediacy of the situation and gain a broader perspective. This can help us avoid decisions driven by momentary emotions or knee-jerk reactions.

During the Observe step of the STOP method, it can be helpful to ask yourself a few key questions: What are the facts of the situation? What emotions am I experiencing right now? What are the potential consequences of this decision, both short-term and long-term? By systematically considering these aspects, we can make more balanced and well-informed decisions.

Another powerful mindful decision-making tool is the body scan. Our bodies often hold wisdom that our busy minds overlook. Before making a significant decision, take a few moments to scan your body from head to toe. Notice any areas of tension, discomfort, or ease. Pay attention to your gut feeling. While this shouldn't be the sole basis for your decision, tuning into your body's wisdom can provide valuable insights that complement your logical analysis.

The body scan technique recognizes that decision making isn't purely a cognitive process. Our emotions and physical sensations play a significant role in how we perceive and respond to situations. By tuning into these bodily cues, we can access a broader range of information to inform our decisions.

When practicing the body scan for decision making, pay particular attention to any physical sensations that arise when you think about different options. Do you feel a sense of expansion or contraction in your chest? Does your stomach tighten or relax? These physical cues can often point to subconscious knowledge or preferences that our conscious mind hasn't yet recognized.

Using intuition mindfully in decision making is a delicate balance. While gut feelings can be valuable, they can also be influenced by biases and past experiences that may not be relevant to the current situation. The key is to acknowledge your intuitive response, but also to examine it critically. Ask yourself: What information or experiences might be informing this gut feeling? Is this intuition relevant to the current situation? By bringing mindful awareness to our intuitive responses, we can harness their power while also maintaining a balanced, rational approach. Intuition can be particularly valuable in complex situations where we're dealing with incomplete information or where there's no clear "right" answer. In these cases, our intuition might be drawing on patterns and experiences that our conscious mind hasn't fully processed. However, it's important to remember that intuition is not infallible and should be considered alongside, not instead of, rational analysis.

To use intuition mindfully, try this exercise: After you've logically analyzed a decision, take a moment to sit quietly and imagine yourself having made each possible choice. Notice how your body and emotions respond to each imagined outcome. This can help you tap into your intuitive wisdom while still maintaining a mindful, observant stance.

Group decision making presents its own set of challenges, but mindfulness can be a powerful tool in this context as well. Before beginning a group decision-making process, consider starting with a brief mindfulness exercise. This could be as simple as a minute of silent breathing together, or a short guided visualization. This shared moment of mindfulness can help align the group's energy and create a more focused, present atmosphere for the discussion.

Group decision making often involves navigating different personalities, opinions, and agendas. Mindfulness can help create a more harmonious and productive decision-making environment by encouraging presence, open-mindedness, and mutual respect among group members. It can also help reduce the impact of groupthink by encouraging each individual to stay connected with their own thoughts and feelings.

When facilitating a mindful group decision-making process, it can be helpful to establish ground rules that support mindful interaction. These might include agreeing to speak one at a time, to listen fully without interrupting, and to pause before responding to others' contributions. These practices can help create a more thoughtful and inclusive decision-making process.

During group discussions, encourage mindful listening. This involves truly hearing what others are saying without immediately formulating a response or judgment. It can be helpful to institute a practice of pausing for a breath between speakers, allowing everyone to fully absorb what has been said before moving on.

Mindful listening in group decision making can lead to more innovative and collaborative outcomes. When we truly listen to others, we open ourselves up to new perspectives and ideas that we might not have considered on our own. This can lead to more robust and well-rounded decisions that take into account a broader range of viewpoints and information.

To further enhance mindful group decision making, consider using techniques like round-robin sharing, where each person has an opportunity to speak without interruption, or silent reflection periods, where group members can quietly consider options before discussing them collectively. These practices can help ensure that all voices are heard and that decisions are made with full consideration of all available input.

As you cultivate mindful decision making in your professional life, you may begin to notice several shifts. You might find that you're less reactive in your choices, able to pause and consider options more fully before acting. You may become more aware of your own biases and how they influence your decisions. You might also notice an increased ability to make decisions in alignment with your values and long-term goals, rather than being swayed by short-term pressures.

This increased self-awareness is a key benefit of mindful decision making. As we become more attuned to our thought processes, emotional responses, and physical sensations, we're better able to recognize when our decisions are being influenced by factors like stress, fear, or unconscious biases. This awareness allows us to make more intentional choices that truly reflect our values and objectives.

You might also find that mindful decision making leads to a greater sense of confidence and peace with your choices. When we've taken the time to consider decisions mindfully, we're less likely to second-guess ourselves or experience decision regret. Even when outcomes aren't what we hoped for, we can feel confident that we made the best decision possible with the information available at the time.

Remember, like all aspects of mindfulness, decision making is a practice. There will be times when you fall back into old patterns of reactive or hasty decision making. The key is to approach each decision as a fresh opportunity to practice mindfulness, learning and growing with each experience.

When you do find yourself making a decision reactively or without mindfulness, treat it as an opportunity for learning rather than a failure. Reflect on what led to the reactive decision. Were you under particular stress? Were you trying to avoid discomfort? Understanding these triggers can help you be more prepared to approach similar situations mindfully in the future.

It can be helpful to regularly review your decision-making process. Perhaps at the end of each week, take some time to reflect on the significant decisions you made. Consider which decisions you feel good about and why. For decisions you're less satisfied with, think about how a more mindful approach might have led to a different outcome. This reflective practice can help you continually refine your mindful decision-making skills.

As we conclude this chapter, consider setting an intention around mindful decision making for your next workday. Perhaps you'll commit to using the STOP method before each significant decision, or to taking a mindful pause before your next team decision-making session. Whatever you choose, approach it with curiosity and openness.

Remember that becoming a mindful decision-maker is a journey, not a destination. Each decision is an opportunity to practice and grow. Be patient with yourself as you develop this skill, and celebrate the small victories along the way.

Your journey towards becoming a more mindful professional continues with each thoughtful choice and each moment of clarity in the face of complexity. As you move forward, remain curious about your decision-making processes. Notice how different approaches affect the quality of your decisions and your overall satisfaction with the outcomes. And above all, trust in your growing capacity to navigate complex choices with mindfulness and wisdom.

CHAPTER 9: MINDFULNESS FOR LEADERSHIP: CULTIVATING PRESENCE AND VISION

In the realm of professional leadership, the ability to navigate complex challenges, inspire teams, and drive innovation is paramount. Yet, in the face of constant pressures and rapidly changing business landscapes, many leaders find themselves operating on autopilot, reacting to crises rather than proactively shaping their organization's future. Mindfulness offers a powerful tool for leaders to cultivate the presence, emotional intelligence, and visionary thinking needed to excel in today's dynamic business environment.

The modern business world is characterized by volatility, uncertainty, complexity, and ambiguity (VUCA). In this context, traditional leadership approaches that rely on rigid hierarchies and top-down decision-making are often inadequate. Leaders are called upon to be agile, adaptable, and innovative, all while maintaining a steady hand on the helm of their organizations. This is where mindfulness can play a crucial role, offering leaders a way to stay grounded and focused amidst the chaos of rapid change and competing demands.

Moreover, the expectations placed on leaders have evolved. Today's workforce, particularly younger generations, are looking for more than just a paycheck. They seek purpose, meaning, and a sense of connection in their work. They expect leaders to be not just competent managers, but also inspirational figures who can articulate a compelling vision and create an environment where individuals can thrive. Mindful leadership addresses these expectations by fostering a more holistic, human-centered approach to leadership.

The mindful leader is characterized by a unique set of qualities that set them apart in the professional world. At the core of mindful leadership is presence – the ability to be fully engaged in the current moment, aware of oneself and others without distraction or judgment. This presence allows leaders to listen more deeply, respond more effectively to challenges, and make decisions with greater clarity and purpose.

Presence in leadership goes beyond simply being physically present. It involves bringing one's full attention and awareness to each interaction, each decision, each moment of the day. When a leader is truly present, team members feel heard and valued. Meetings become more productive as the leader's focused attention encourages others to engage more fully. Decision-making improves as the leader is able to take in and process information more effectively, without the distortion of preconceived notions or habitual reactions.

Cultivating presence as a leader involves regular mindfulness practice. This might include formal meditation sessions, but it also extends to bringing mindful awareness to everyday leadership activities. For example, before entering a meeting, a mindful leader might take a few deep breaths to center themselves and set an intention for the interaction. During conversations, they practice active listening, giving their full attention to the speaker rather than allowing their mind to wander to other concerns.

Mindful leaders also exhibit a high degree of self-awareness. They are attuned to their own thoughts, emotions, and behaviors, and understand how these impact their leadership style and decisions. This self-awareness extends to an understanding of their own strengths and limitations, allowing them to leverage their talents effectively and seek support or development in areas where they may be less strong.

Self-awareness is a cornerstone of effective leadership, and mindfulness is a powerful tool for developing it. Through mindfulness practices, leaders can become more attuned to their own internal states – their thoughts, emotions, and physical sensations. This heightened self-awareness allows leaders to recognize their own biases, understand their reactive patterns, and make more conscious choices about how to respond to situations.

For example, a mindful leader might notice that they tend to become defensive when receiving criticism. By being aware of this tendency, they can choose to respond differently – perhaps by taking a deep breath and asking for more information instead of immediately reacting. This kind of self-awareness and self-regulation can dramatically improve a leader's effectiveness and the quality of their relationships with team members.

Another key characteristic of mindful leaders is their ability to manage stress and maintain equilibrium in the face of challenges. Through regular mindfulness practice, these leaders develop a greater capacity to respond to difficult situations with calm and clarity, rather than reacting impulsively or becoming overwhelmed.

Leadership roles often come with high levels of stress. The pressure to meet targets, manage team dynamics, and navigate organizational politics can take a toll on a leader's well-being and decision-making capacity. Mindfulness provides leaders with tools to manage this stress effectively. Regular mindfulness practice has been shown to reduce the body's stress response, lower cortisol levels, and improve overall resilience.

When faced with a challenging situation, a mindful leader might pause to take a few deep breaths, grounding themselves in the present moment. This brief pause can create space between the stimulus and the response, allowing the leader to choose a more measured and effective course of action. Over time, this ability to respond rather than react becomes ingrained, leading to more consistent and effective leadership even in high-pressure situations.

The benefits of mindful leadership extend far beyond the individual leader. Organizations led by mindful leaders often experience improved team dynamics, increased employee engagement and well-being, and enhanced overall performance. Mindful leaders create an environment of trust and openness, where creativity can flourish and where team members feel valued and heard.

When leaders model mindfulness, it can have a ripple effect throughout the organization. Team members may begin to adopt more mindful practices in their own work, leading to improved focus, reduced stress, and better collaboration. The overall work environment may become calmer and more positive, with fewer conflicts and more constructive problem-solving.

Research has shown that organizations with mindful leaders tend to have higher levels of employee engagement. This is likely because mindful leaders are more attuned to their team members' needs and concerns, and are better able to create an environment where people feel valued and motivated. Higher engagement, in turn, leads to improved productivity, lower turnover rates, and better overall organizational performance.

Developing emotional intelligence through mindfulness is a crucial aspect of effective leadership. Emotional intelligence encompasses the ability to recognize and manage one's own emotions, as well as the capacity to understand and influence the emotions of others. Mindfulness practices can significantly enhance emotional intelligence by increasing our awareness of our own emotional states and improving our ability to recognize emotions in others.

Emotional intelligence is often cited as one of the most important qualities for effective leadership. It allows leaders to navigate complex interpersonal dynamics, motivate and inspire their teams, and make decisions that take into account the human element of business. Mindfulness enhances emotional intelligence by developing the capacity for self-awareness and self-regulation, two key components of EI.

Moreover, mindfulness practices can improve a leader's ability to empathize with others. By becoming more attuned to their own emotional states, leaders become better able to recognize and understand the emotions of those around them. This enhanced empathy can lead to more effective communication, better conflict resolution, and stronger relationships with team members and stakeholders.

To develop emotional intelligence through mindfulness, start by incorporating regular check-ins throughout your day. Take a moment to pause and notice your emotional state. What are you feeling? How is this emotion manifesting in your body? How might it be influencing your thoughts and behaviors? As you become more aware of your own emotions, you'll likely find that you become more attuned to the emotional states of those around you as well.

These emotional check-ins can be brief – even just a minute or two – but they can have a powerful impact on your leadership effectiveness. By regularly tuning into your emotional state, you can catch potential issues before they escalate. For example, you might notice that you're feeling irritable due to lack of sleep, and choose to postpone an important meeting until you're in a better state of mind.

As you practice these check-ins, you may also start to notice patterns in your emotional responses to different situations. Perhaps you tend to feel anxious before board meetings, or frustrated when dealing with a particular team member. Recognizing these patterns allows you to prepare more effectively, perhaps by doing some deep breathing exercises before anxiety-provoking situations or by planning extra time for patience when dealing with challenging interpersonal dynamics.

Mindful approaches to conflict resolution can transform the way leaders handle disagreements and tensions within their teams. Instead of viewing conflict as a problem to be avoided, mindful leaders see it as an opportunity for growth and deeper understanding. When faced with a conflict situation, take a moment to center yourself with a few deep breaths. Approach the situation with curiosity rather than judgment, seeking to understand all perspectives involved. Practice active listening, giving each party your full attention and reflecting back what you've heard to ensure understanding.

Conflict is inevitable in any organization, but how leaders handle conflict can make the difference between a dysfunctional team and a high-performing one. Mindful conflict resolution involves staying present and non-reactive in the face of disagreement or tension. It means listening deeply to all parties involved, seeking to understand not just the surface-level disagreement but the underlying needs and concerns that are driving the conflict.

A mindful approach to conflict also involves recognizing and managing one's own emotional responses to the situation. Leaders who can remain calm and centered during conflicts are better able to guide their teams towards constructive solutions. They can model effective communication and problem-solving skills, helping to create a culture where conflicts are seen as opportunities for growth and innovation rather than sources of stress and division.

Creating a mindful organizational culture is perhaps one of the most impactful ways that leaders can leverage mindfulness.

This involves more than just offering meditation classes or mindfulness workshops (although these can be valuable). It's about infusing mindfulness principles into the very fabric of how the organization operates.

A mindful organizational culture is one where reflection and intentionality are valued alongside action and results. It's a culture where employees are encouraged to take regular breaks to recharge, where meetings begin with a moment of centering, and where mindful communication practices are the norm rather than the exception. In such a culture, creativity and innovation can flourish because people feel psychologically safe to express new ideas and take calculated risks.

Creating this kind of culture requires consistent effort and modeling from leadership. It's not enough to simply advocate for mindfulness – leaders must embody these principles in their own behavior and decision-making. This might involve making visible changes to how you operate as a leader, such as instituting "no-meeting" days to allow for focused work time, or starting team meetings with a brief mindfulness exercise.

Start by modeling mindful behavior yourself. Be present in your interactions, practice active listening, and demonstrate a balanced approach to work and well-being. Encourage mindful communication practices in meetings and email exchanges. Create spaces for reflection and quiet work within the office environment. Recognize and reward not just results, but also thoughtful processes and collaborative behaviors.

Consider implementing specific practices that support a mindful culture. For example, you might introduce a "mindful minute" at the beginning of meetings, where everyone takes a moment to breathe and center themselves before diving into the agenda. Or you could create a quiet room in the office where employees can go to meditate or simply take a few moments of silence during their workday.

It's also important to align your organization's policies and procedures with mindfulness principles. This might involve revisiting your approach to performance evaluations to include measures of collaboration and mindful leadership. Or it could mean adjusting work schedules to allow for more flexibility and work-life balance.

Mindfulness can be a powerful tool for strategic thinking and innovation. By cultivating a clear and focused mind, leaders can cut through the noise of day-to-day operations and tap into more creative and visionary thinking. Regular mindfulness practice can help leaders step back from immediate concerns and consider the bigger picture, identifying emerging trends and opportunities that others might miss.

Strategic thinking requires the ability to zoom out from day-to-day concerns and consider the long-term direction of the organization. However, the constant demands of leadership can make it challenging to find the mental space for this kind of big-picture thinking. Mindfulness practices can help create this space by training the mind to let go of distractions and focus on what's truly important.

Moreover, mindfulness can enhance creativity and innovation by fostering a state of open awareness. In this state, leaders are more receptive to new ideas and perspectives, and more able to make novel connections between disparate concepts. This can lead to breakthrough insights and innovative solutions to complex problems.

To leverage mindfulness for strategic thinking, try incorporating regular "strategic pauses" into your schedule. These might be brief daily reflection periods or longer weekly or monthly sessions where you step away from operational tasks to focus on bigger-picture thinking. During these times, use mindfulness techniques to clear your mind and create space for new ideas and perspectives to emerge.

These strategic pauses could take various forms. You might start your day with a 10-minute meditation focused on your organization's mission and long-term goals. Or you could schedule a monthly "strategy walk," where you leave your office and take a mindful walk in nature, allowing your mind to wander and make new connections. The key is to create regular opportunities to step back from the day-to-day and engage in more expansive thinking.

During these strategic pauses, practice open awareness. Instead of trying to force solutions or ideas, allow your mind to relax and see what emerges. You might be surprised by the insights that arise when you create space for them. Keep a journal nearby to capture any ideas or insights that come up during these sessions.

As you incorporate these mindful leadership practices into your professional life, you may begin to notice shifts in both your own leadership style and in the dynamics of your team or organization. You might find that you're able to navigate complex challenges with greater ease, that your team becomes more cohesive and innovative, or that you're able to maintain a clearer vision of your long-term goals even amidst day-to-day pressures.

These changes often happen gradually, so it's important to be patient and consistent in your practice. You might start to notice small shifts first – perhaps you're better able to stay calm during a crisis, or you find yourself listening more attentively in meetings. Over time, these small changes can add up to significant transformations in your leadership effectiveness and your organization's culture.

Pay attention to feedback from your team and colleagues. They may notice changes in your leadership style before you do. Are they commenting that you seem more present or approachable? Do they feel more heard and valued? These can be important indicators that your mindful leadership practices are having a positive impact.

Remember, mindful leadership is not about achieving a state of perfect calm or eliminating all stress and conflict. Rather, it's about developing the capacity to be present, aware, and intentional in your role as a leader. It's about cultivating the wisdom to know when to act and when to pause, when to speak and when to listen, when to push forward and when to step back.

Mindful leadership is a journey, not a destination. There will be days when you feel fully present and effective, and others when you struggle to maintain your mindful intentions. The key is to approach each day, each interaction, each challenge with renewed commitment to your practice. Even in moments when you fall short of your ideals, the awareness that comes from mindfulness allows you to recognize these moments and learn from them.

As you continue on this journey, consider seeking support and community. This might involve finding a mindfulness mentor, joining a leadership group focused on mindful practices, or even starting a mindfulness initiative within your own organization. Sharing your experiences and learning from others can be a powerful way to deepen your practice and stay motivated.

As we conclude this chapter, consider setting an intention for how you might bring more mindfulness into your leadership practice. Perhaps you'll commit to starting each day with a brief meditation, or to practicing active listening in your next team meeting. Maybe you'll introduce a mindful pause at the beginning of your next board meeting, or schedule regular strategic reflection time in your calendar.

Whatever you choose, approach it with openness and curiosity. Be willing to experiment and adjust your approach based on what you learn. Remember that becoming a mindful leader is an ongoing process of growth and discovery. Each day brings new opportunities to practice presence, cultivate awareness, and lead with intention.

Your journey towards becoming a more mindful leader continues with each present moment and each intentional action. As you move forward, remain curious about your experiences. Notice how your mindful practices impact your decision-making, your relationships with team members, and your overall effectiveness as a leader. And above all, be kind to yourself as you navigate this path. The challenges of leadership are many, but with mindfulness as your foundation, you have a powerful tool for meeting these challenges with clarity, compassion, and vision.

CHAPTER 10: DIGITAL MINDFULNESS: NAVIGATING THE ALWAYS-ON WORLD

In today's professional landscape, digital technology is ubiquitous. From smartphones and laptops to cloud-based collaboration tools and social media platforms, we are more connected than ever before. While these technologies offer unprecedented opportunities for communication, productivity, and innovation, they also present significant challenges to our attention, well-being, and work-life balance. The concept of digital mindfulness emerges as a crucial skill for navigating this always-on world, allowing us to harness the benefits of technology while mitigating its potential drawbacks.

The digital revolution has transformed the way we work, communicate, and live. It has brought about remarkable advancements in efficiency and connectivity, enabling us to accomplish tasks that were once unimaginable. We can collaborate with colleagues across the globe in real-time, access vast amounts of information at our fingertips, and automate repetitive tasks to focus on more creative and strategic work.

However, this digital transformation has also introduced new challenges that we must learn to navigate mindfully.

One of the most significant challenges of our digital age is the blurring of boundaries between work and personal life. With our devices always within reach, it's become increasingly difficult to truly "clock out" at the end of the workday. Emails, instant messages, and work-related notifications can intrude on our personal time, making it challenging to fully relax and recharge. This constant connectivity can lead to a sense of always being "on call," which can contribute to stress, anxiety, and eventual burnout.

The impact of digital overload on focus and well-being cannot be overstated. Constant connectivity can lead to a state of continuous partial attention, where we're never fully engaged in any single task or interaction. This fragmented attention not only reduces our productivity but also increases stress levels and can contribute to burnout. Moreover, the blue light emitted by our devices can disrupt our sleep patterns, further impacting our overall well-being and cognitive function.

The phenomenon of continuous partial attention was first described by Linda Stone, a former Apple and Microsoft executive. It refers to a state where we're constantly scanning our environment for new information or stimuli, never fully focusing on any one thing. In our digital work environments, this might manifest as constantly checking email while working on a project, or half-listening to a virtual meeting while simultaneously browsing the internet. While this behavior might feel productive in the moment, it actually reduces our ability to think deeply, solve complex problems, and engage meaningfully with our work and colleagues.

Furthermore, the constant influx of information and stimuli from our digital devices can overwhelm our cognitive capacities. The human brain, while remarkably adaptable, was not designed to process the sheer volume of information we encounter in our digital lives. This information overload can lead to decision fatigue, reduced creativity, and difficulty in distinguishing between important and trivial information.

To combat digital overload, start by bringing awareness to your technology use. Take a "digital inventory" of your typical workday. Notice how often you check your email, how frequently you switch between tasks or applications, and how much time you spend on social media or other potentially distracting platforms. This awareness is the first step in developing a more mindful approach to technology use.

Conducting a digital inventory can be an eye-opening experience. You might be surprised to discover just how often you reach for your phone or switch between applications. To make this process more structured, consider using a time-tracking app for a week to get an accurate picture of your digital habits. Pay attention not just to the quantity of time spent on different digital activities, but also to the quality of that time. Are you using technology in ways that align with your goals and values, or are you often getting sidetracked by digital distractions?

As you conduct your digital inventory, also notice the emotional and physical impact of your technology use. Do you feel energized after certain digital activities, or drained? Do you experience physical tension or discomfort after prolonged device use? Understanding these effects can help motivate you to make changes and develop more mindful digital habits.

Once you've gained awareness of your digital habits, you can begin to implement strategies for more mindful use of social media and email. One effective approach is to designate specific times for checking and responding to emails, rather than constantly monitoring your inbox. This allows you to focus more deeply on other tasks without the constant interruption of incoming messages.

The practice of "batching" emails – checking and responding to them in dedicated blocks of time rather than continuously throughout the day – can significantly improve your productivity and reduce stress. Consider setting two or three specific times during your workday for email management. Outside of these times, close your email application or turn off notifications to minimize distractions. This approach allows you to be more intentional and focused in your email communications, rather than reactive.

When you do check your email, approach it mindfully. Before opening your inbox, take a few deep breaths and set an intention for how you want to engage with your messages. As you read and respond to emails, stay present with the task at hand rather than letting your mind wander to other concerns. If you notice yourself becoming stressed or overwhelmed by your inbox, pause and take a moment to recenter yourself before continuing.

For social media, consider setting clear boundaries around its use during work hours. If you need to use social media for professional purposes, try using website blockers or apps that limit your access to specific platforms outside of designated times. When you do engage with social media, do so mindfully. Before posting or responding to a message, take a breath and consider your intention. Is this communication necessary and beneficial?

Social media, while a powerful tool for networking and information sharing, can also be a significant source of distraction and stress in our professional lives. It's easy to fall into the trap of mindless scrolling, comparing ourselves to others, or getting caught up in online debates that drain our energy and attention. To use social media more mindfully, try implementing a "social media budget" – allotting a specific amount of time each day for social media use and sticking to it.

When you do engage with social media, do so with intention and awareness. Before logging on, ask yourself what you hope to achieve or gain from this interaction. As you scroll, post, or comment, stay aware of your emotional state. If you notice that your social media use is causing stress, anxiety, or negative self-comparison, it may be time to reassess your relationship with these platforms.

Digital detox strategies can be powerful tools for professionals seeking to regain balance in their relationship with technology. While a complete "unplugging" may not be feasible for many of us, even short periods of digital disconnection can have significant benefits. Consider implementing a "tech-free" hour each day, perhaps during your lunch break or in the evening after work. Use this time to engage in non-digital activities such as reading, exercising, or connecting face-to-face with colleagues or loved ones.

The concept of a digital detox doesn't mean completely abandoning technology, but rather creating intentional periods of disconnection to recharge and reconnect with the non-digital world. These breaks can help reset our relationship with technology and remind us that we are in control of our devices, not the other way around. During your tech-free periods, you might be surprised to find that your mind feels clearer, your stress levels decrease, and you're able to engage more fully with your surroundings and the people around you.

To make digital detox a regular part of your routine, try starting small. Perhaps begin with a tech-free meal each day, where you put away all devices and focus solely on your food and any companions. Gradually increase the duration of your tech-free periods as you become more comfortable with disconnecting. You might also consider designating certain spaces in your home or office as "tech-free zones" to create physical boundaries around your digital use.

Weekends or vacations can offer opportunities for longer periods of digital detox. If possible, try leaving your work devices at home when you go on vacation, or designate specific, limited times for checking in with work. You may find that these periods of disconnection allow for greater relaxation, creativity, and perspective.

Taking a more extended digital detox during vacations or weekends can be particularly rejuvenating. It allows us to fully disconnect from work pressures and immerse ourselves in rest and recreation. However, the prospect of being completely disconnected can also cause anxiety, especially if we're used to being constantly available. To ease into longer periods of digital detox, try setting clear expectations with colleagues before your time off. Let them know when you'll be unavailable and who they can contact in your absence. This can help alleviate the fear of missing out or letting others down.

During your digital detox periods, pay attention to how you feel. You might initially experience some discomfort or restlessness – this is normal and often a sign of how dependent we've become on our devices. As you persist, however, you may notice increased feelings of calm, improved ability to focus on the present moment, and a renewed appreciation for face-to-face interactions and non-digital activities.

Mindful approaches to virtual meetings and remote work have become increasingly important in our digital age, particularly in the wake of global shifts towards remote and hybrid work models. When participating in virtual meetings, practice being fully present. Close unnecessary browser tabs and applications to minimize distractions. Turn off notifications on your phone or computer. If possible, use a "gallery view" that allows you to see all participants, helping you stay engaged with the group.

Virtual meetings, while convenient, can also be a source of stress and fatigue. The phenomenon of "Zoom fatigue" has become well-recognized, referring to the mental exhaustion that can result from prolonged video conferencing. To combat this, try implementing mindful practices before, during, and after your virtual meetings. Before joining a call, take a few moments to center yourself. Take some deep breaths, set an intention for the meeting, and prepare your space to minimize distractions.

During virtual meetings, practice active listening. Really focus on what others are saying, rather than planning your response or multitasking. If you find your mind wandering, gently bring your attention back to the present moment. Be aware of your own presence on the call – are you fully engaged, or are you showing up as distracted or disinterested? Remember that your facial expressions and body language are visible to others, even in a virtual setting.

Before joining a virtual meeting, take a moment to center yourself. Take a few deep breaths and set an intention for your participation. After the meeting, allow yourself a brief transition period before jumping into the next task. This might involve a short stretching break or a few minutes of mindful breathing.

These transition periods between virtual meetings are crucial for maintaining focus and preventing burnout. It can be tempting to schedule back-to-back video calls, but this leaves no time for processing information, making notes, or simply giving our minds a break. Try scheduling meetings for 25 or 50 minutes instead of 30 or 60, using the extra time as a buffer for transitions. During these breaks, stand up and move your body, look away from your screen to rest your eyes, or practice a brief mindfulness exercise to reset your attention.

For remote work more broadly, creating clear boundaries between work and personal time is crucial. Designate a specific workspace in your home if possible, and try to confine work activities to this space. Establish a routine that includes clear start and end times for your workday, including regular breaks. Use transition rituals, such as a short walk or meditation, to mark the shift between work and personal time.

Working from home can blur the lines between professional and personal life, making it challenging to "switch off" at the end of the workday. To maintain a healthy work-life balance in a remote setting, try creating a "fake commute" – a ritual that marks the beginning and end of your workday. This could involve taking a short walk around your neighborhood, doing a brief meditation, or engaging in any activity that helps you transition mentally between work and personal time.

Be mindful of your work environment when working remotely. Try to create a space that is conducive to focus and productivity, but also comfortable. Pay attention to ergonomics to prevent physical strain from prolonged computer use. Consider incorporating elements that promote mindfulness into your workspace, such as plants, calming colors, or objects that inspire you.

While technology can present challenges to mindfulness, it can also be leveraged to support mindfulness practice. There are numerous apps and online platforms that offer guided meditations, mindfulness exercises, and tools for tracking your practice. Some apps even provide gentle reminders throughout the day to take mindful breaks or check in with your breath.

When choosing mindfulness apps or digital tools, be selective. It's easy to fall into the trap of downloading multiple apps and then feeling overwhelmed by the options. Start with one or two that resonate with you and commit to using them regularly. Remember that the app itself is just a tool – the real work of mindfulness happens in your own mind and body.

Consider how you can use technology to create mindful habits rather than distracted ones. For example, you might use your smartphone's alarm function to remind you to take regular mindful breaks throughout your workday. Or you could use a habit-tracking app to monitor your progress with mindfulness practices like meditation or journaling.

Wearable devices can be used to monitor stress levels and prompt you to take breaks or engage in brief mindfulness exercises when your stress indicators are high. Digital calendars can be used to schedule regular mindfulness breaks throughout your day.

While wearable devices and health-tracking apps can provide valuable data, it's important to use this information mindfully. Pay attention to how tracking your health metrics affects your stress levels and overall well-being. For some people, constant monitoring can increase anxiety rather than reduce it. Use these tools in a way that supports your mindfulness practice rather than detracts from it.

When using digital calendars to schedule mindfulness breaks, treat these appointments with the same respect you would any other important meeting. It can be tempting to skip scheduled breaks when work pressures mount, but remember that these moments of mindfulness can actually improve your productivity and decision-making in the long run.

As you incorporate these digital mindfulness practices into your professional life, you may begin to notice shifts in your relationship with technology. You might find that you're able to use digital tools more intentionally and effectively, without feeling controlled by them. You may experience improved focus and productivity during work hours, and a greater ability to disconnect and relax during personal time.

These changes often happen gradually, so be patient with yourself as you develop new habits. You might start to notice small shifts first – perhaps you feel less compelled to check your email constantly, or you find it easier to focus on one task at a time without the urge to multitask. Over time, these small changes can add up to a significant transformation in your relationship with technology.

Pay attention to how your digital mindfulness practices affect your overall well-being. Are you sleeping better? Do you feel less stressed at the end of the workday? Are you able to be more present in your personal relationships? These broader impacts can provide motivation to continue and deepen your digital mindfulness practice.

Remember, the goal of digital mindfulness is not to eliminate technology from our lives, but to cultivate a more balanced and intentional relationship with it. It's about using technology as a tool to enhance our work and lives, rather than allowing it to drive our behavior and attention.

This balanced approach recognizes that technology is an integral and valuable part of our professional lives. The aim is not to demonize digital tools, but to use them in a way that aligns with our goals and values. This might mean embracing certain technologies that genuinely improve our work or life, while setting boundaries around others that tend to distract or drain us.

As you continue to practice digital mindfulness, you may find that your discernment about technology use improves. You might become more selective about which digital tools you adopt, choosing only those that truly add value to your work and life. You may also find that you're better able to recognize when technology is enhancing your productivity and well-being, and when it's detracting from it.

As we conclude this chapter, consider setting an intention for how you might bring more mindfulness to your digital life. Perhaps you'll commit to implementing regular tech-free breaks, or to practicing more mindful engagement with email and social media. Whatever you choose, approach it with curiosity and compassion for yourself.

Start small and be patient with yourself as you develop new habits. Remember that changing ingrained digital behaviors takes time and practice. If you find yourself slipping back into old patterns, treat it as an opportunity for learning rather than a failure. Notice what triggered the slip and use that information to refine your approach.

Consider sharing your digital mindfulness journey with colleagues or friends. You might find that others are experiencing similar challenges and are interested in exploring more mindful approaches to technology use. Sharing experiences and strategies can provide valuable support and accountability as you develop new habits.

Your journey towards becoming a more mindful professional in the digital age continues with each conscious click, each intentional response, and each moment of digital presence. As you move forward, remain curious about your relationship with technology. Notice how different digital habits affect your productivity, your stress levels, and your overall satisfaction with your work and life. And above all, remember that you have the power to shape your digital environment in a way that supports your well-being and professional success.

CHAPTER 11: CREATING YOUR PERSONALIZED MINDFULNESS PRACTICE

As we near the conclusion of our exploration into mindfulness for the busy professional, it's time to turn our attention to perhaps the most crucial aspect of this journey: creating a personalized mindfulness practice that fits seamlessly into your unique lifestyle and professional demands. While the principles and techniques we've discussed throughout this book provide a strong foundation, the true power of mindfulness emerges when it's tailored to your individual needs, preferences, and circumstances.

The process of developing a personal mindfulness practice is both an art and a science. It requires a balance of structure and flexibility, discipline and creativity. This personalization is critical because what works for one person may not work for another. Our lives, work environments, personalities, and challenges are all unique, and our mindfulness practice should reflect this individuality.

Moreover, a personalized practice is more likely to be sustainable in the long term. When we create a practice that aligns with our lifestyle and resonates with our values, we're more likely to stick with it, even when faced with the inevitable challenges and distractions of professional life. This sustainability is key to reaping the full benefits of mindfulness over time.

The first step in creating your personalized mindfulness practice is to assess your current mindfulness level. This isn't about judging yourself or striving for some idealized state of enlightenment. Rather, it's about honestly reflecting on your current relationship with mindfulness and identifying areas where you'd like to grow. Consider questions such as: How often do you find yourself fully present in the moment? How easily do you get distracted or overwhelmed during your workday? How well do you manage stress and emotional challenges?

This self-assessment serves multiple purposes. First, it provides a baseline from which you can measure your progress. Second, it helps you identify specific areas where mindfulness could be particularly beneficial in your professional life. Perhaps you notice that you struggle with staying focused during long meetings, or that you often react impulsively to stressful emails. These observations can guide you in choosing mindfulness techniques that address your particular challenges.

When conducting this self-assessment, try to approach it with curiosity rather than judgment. The goal is not to criticize yourself for not being "mindful enough," but to gain insights that can inform your practice. Remember, everyone starts their mindfulness journey from where they are, and recognizing your starting point is an important step in the process.

You might find it helpful to keep a mindfulness journal for a week, noting moments when you felt particularly present or mindful, as well as times when you struggled with distraction or stress. This self-reflection can provide valuable insights into your current mindfulness baseline and help you identify specific areas for focus in your practice.

In your mindfulness journal, consider noting not just what happened, but also how you felt and responded in different situations. For example, you might write about a challenging interaction with a colleague, noting how present you were during the conversation, what emotions arose, and how you managed them. Or you could reflect on a period of focused work, describing what helped you maintain concentration and what distractions you encountered.

This journaling process can reveal patterns and triggers that you might not have been aware of. Perhaps you notice that you're most mindful early in the morning, or that certain types of tasks consistently challenge your ability to stay present. These insights can be invaluable as you design your personalized practice.

Setting realistic goals for your practice is crucial for long-term success. It's easy to get excited about mindfulness and set ambitious goals, but this enthusiasm can quickly wane when faced with the realities of a busy professional life. Instead, start small and build gradually. Perhaps your initial goal is to practice five minutes of mindful breathing each morning before work. Or maybe you aim to incorporate one mindful eating experience into your day. Whatever goals you set, make sure they are specific, measurable, and achievable within your current lifestyle.

When setting goals for your mindfulness practice, consider using the SMART framework: Specific, Measurable, Achievable, Relevant, and Time-bound. For example, instead of a vague goal like "be more mindful at work," you might set a SMART goal such as "Practice 5 minutes of mindful breathing at my desk before starting work each day for the next month."

It's also important to set goals that are meaningful to you personally. Consider what aspects of mindfulness you're most drawn to, or what benefits you're hoping to gain from your practice. Are you looking to reduce stress, improve focus, enhance creativity, or develop better relationships with colleagues? Aligning your goals with your personal motivations can help you stay committed to your practice.

Remember, consistency is more important than duration when it comes to mindfulness practice. A brief daily practice will likely yield more benefits than sporadic longer sessions. As you become more comfortable with your practice, you can gradually increase its duration or frequency.

The power of consistency in mindfulness practice cannot be overstated. Regular, even if brief, engagement with mindfulness techniques allows the brain to form new neural pathways, gradually rewiring our habitual responses to stress and enhancing our capacity for presence and awareness. This neuroplasticity is key to experiencing the long-term benefits of mindfulness in our professional lives.

As you develop your practice, be prepared for ebbs and flows in your motivation and consistency. There may be periods where your practice feels effortless and rewarding, and others where it feels challenging to maintain. This is normal and part of the process. The key is to approach these fluctuations with self-compassion and to gently recommit to your practice when you notice you've drifted away from it.

Choosing techniques that resonate with you is key to developing a sustainable mindfulness practice. Throughout this book, we've explored a wide range of mindfulness techniques, from basic breathing exercises to more advanced practices like body scans and loving-kindness meditation. Reflect on which of these techniques you found most engaging or beneficial. Which ones seemed to fit most naturally into your daily routine?

When selecting techniques, consider both your personal preferences and your practical constraints. Some people find movement-based practices like mindful walking or yoga most engaging, while others prefer seated meditation or breathing exercises. Some techniques may be more suitable for your work environment than others. For example, a body scan might be challenging to practice in an open office, but a brief mindful breathing exercise could be easily incorporated into your workday.

Also, consider the specific challenges you face in your professional life. If you struggle with emotional regulation, practices that focus on acknowledging and accepting emotions might be particularly beneficial. If you often feel disconnected from your body due to long hours at a desk, body-based mindfulness practices could be especially helpful.

Don't feel pressured to adopt every technique we've discussed. It's perfectly fine, and often more effective, to focus on a few core practices that really speak to you. You might find that mindful breathing works well as a quick reset throughout your workday, while a body scan helps you unwind in the evening. Or perhaps mindful walking resonates with you as a way to transition between work and home life.

As you experiment with different techniques, pay attention to how each practice makes you feel, both during and after. Does it leave you feeling energized and focused, or calm and grounded? Does it feel like a chore, or do you look forward to it? These responses can guide you in selecting the practices that are most beneficial and sustainable for you.

Remember that your preferences may change over time, and that's okay. What works for you now may not be as effective or appealing in the future. Be open to revisiting different techniques and adjusting your practice as needed. The goal is to cultivate a flexible, evolving practice that continues to serve you throughout your professional journey.

Overcoming common obstacles to consistent practice is an important consideration as you develop your personalized approach. Time constraints are often cited as the biggest barrier to maintaining a mindfulness practice. To address this, look for ways to integrate mindfulness into your existing routine rather than trying to carve out large chunks of additional time. This might involve practicing mindful breathing during your commute, bringing awareness to your body as you walk between meetings, or using your lunch break for a brief meditation.

The key to overcoming time constraints is to shift your perspective on what constitutes a "valid" mindfulness practice. While longer, formal meditation sessions can be beneficial, they're not the only way to cultivate mindfulness. Brief moments of presence scattered throughout your day can be just as powerful. These "mindfulness snacks" can add up to a significant practice over time.

Consider identifying "transition points" in your day where you can naturally incorporate brief mindfulness practices. These might include the moment you arrive at your desk in the morning, the time just before or after a meeting, or the period between finishing work and starting your evening routine. Using these transition points as mindfulness cues can help you build a consistent practice without feeling like you're adding extra tasks to your day.

Another common obstacle is forgetting to practice. In our busy lives, it's easy for mindfulness to slip off our radar. Consider using reminders or cues in your environment to prompt your practice. This could be as simple as setting alarms on your phone or placing Post-it notes in strategic locations. Some people find it helpful to link their mindfulness practice to existing habits, such as practicing mindful breathing right after brushing their teeth in the morning.

Visual cues can be particularly effective reminders for mindfulness practice. You might place a small object on your desk that reminds you to take mindful breaks, or set a mindfulness-related image as your computer or phone background. The key is to choose reminders that are noticeable enough to catch your attention, but not so intrusive that they become easy to ignore.

It can also be helpful to enlist the support of colleagues or family members in reminding you to practice. Perhaps you could agree with a coworker to prompt each other to take mindful breaks, or ask your partner to gently remind you about your evening meditation. Having this external support can be especially valuable as you're establishing your practice.

Distractions and wandering thoughts are inevitable parts of any mindfulness practice. Rather than seeing these as failures, try to view them as opportunities to practice returning your attention to the present moment. Each time you notice your mind has wandered and bring it back, you're strengthening your mindfulness "muscle."

It's important to understand that the goal of mindfulness is not to eliminate thoughts or achieve a state of blank-mind calm. Rather, it's about developing the ability to notice our thoughts without getting caught up in them. When you notice your mind wandering during practice, simply acknowledge the thought or distraction without judgment, and gently guide your attention back to your chosen focus, whether that's your breath, your body sensations, or the task at hand.

In fact, the process of noticing that your mind has wandered and bringing it back is the very essence of mindfulness practice. It's this repeated act of returning to the present moment that builds our capacity for focus and presence over time. So rather than feeling frustrated when you get distracted, try to appreciate these moments as valuable opportunities for practice.

Tracking progress and adjusting your approach is essential for maintaining motivation and ensuring your practice continues to serve you effectively. Consider keeping a mindfulness log where you note the duration and type of practice you engage in each day, along with any observations or insights. You might also track relevant metrics such as stress levels, sleep quality, or work productivity to see how your mindfulness practice is impacting different areas of your life.

When tracking your progress, it's important to look beyond just the quantitative aspects of your practice (like duration or frequency) and also consider qualitative changes. Are you noticing increased moments of presence throughout your day? Are you responding to stressful situations differently? Are you experiencing improved relationships with colleagues? These subtle shifts can be powerful indicators of your growing mindfulness.

Remember that progress in mindfulness practice isn't always linear. You may experience periods of significant growth followed by plateaus or even temporary setbacks. This is normal and part of the process. The key is to maintain a consistent practice and to view challenges as opportunities for learning and growth.

Regular review of your practice is important. Perhaps once a month, take some time to reflect on your mindfulness journey. What's working well? What challenges are you facing? Are there areas of your life where you'd like to bring more mindfulness? Use these reflections to make adjustments to your practice as needed. Remember, your mindfulness practice should evolve as your life and work circumstances change.

These regular reviews can help you stay aligned with your goals and ensure that your practice continues to serve you effectively. They're also an opportunity to celebrate your progress and acknowledge the effort you've put into developing your mindfulness skills. Even small improvements are worth recognizing, as they can provide motivation to continue your practice.

During these reviews, be open to making adjustments to your practice. Perhaps you'll decide to try a new technique, increase the duration of your practice, or shift the time of day when you practice. The key is to remain flexible and responsive to your changing needs and circumstances.

As you embark on creating your personalized mindfulness practice, approach the process with curiosity and self-compassion. There's no one "right" way to practice mindfulness. What matters is finding an approach that feels authentic and sustainable for you. Be patient with yourself as you explore different techniques and establish new habits. Celebrate small victories and be gentle with yourself when you face setbacks.

Cultivating self-compassion is particularly important in mindfulness practice. It's easy to become self-critical when we perceive that we're not "doing it right" or not making progress quickly enough. Remember that every moment of practice, regardless of how it feels, is valuable. Each time you choose to be mindful, even for a brief moment, you're strengthening your capacity for presence and awareness.

As you develop your practice, you may find it helpful to connect with others who are on a similar journey. This could involve joining a mindfulness group at your workplace, participating in online forums or communities focused on mindfulness, or simply sharing your experiences with interested colleagues or friends. Having this support and sense of community can provide encouragement, accountability, and valuable insights as you navigate your mindfulness journey.

Your mindfulness practice is a journey, not a destination. It's about cultivating a way of being in the world that allows you to navigate your professional and personal life with greater ease, clarity, and purpose. As you continue to develop and refine your practice, you may find that mindfulness becomes less of a separate activity and more of an integral part of how you approach each moment of your day.

This integration of mindfulness into your daily life is often described as "informal practice." While formal meditation sessions are valuable, it's this moment-to-moment mindfulness that can truly transform your experience of work and life. You might find yourself naturally taking a few mindful breaths before responding to a challenging email, or bringing full awareness to a conversation with a colleague without consciously deciding to "practice mindfulness."

As your practice deepens, you may also notice ripple effects in various areas of your professional life. You might find that you're better able to manage stress, that your decision-making becomes more clear and intentional, or that your relationships with colleagues improve. These positive changes can provide powerful motivation to continue and deepen your practice.

As we conclude this chapter, take a moment to set an intention for your personalized mindfulness practice. What do you hope to gain from this practice? How do you envision it enhancing your professional life? With this intention in mind, commit to taking the first step in creating your practice, however small it may be. Your journey towards becoming a more mindful professional continues with each conscious breath, each moment of presence, and each intentional step on this path of self-discovery and growth.

Remember that this intention is not set in stone. It can evolve as you progress in your practice and as your needs and circumstances change. The important thing is to have a clear sense of purpose as you begin, something that can guide and motivate you as you develop your personalized mindfulness practice.

As you move forward, approach each day as a new opportunity to bring mindfulness into your professional life. Even on days when formal practice feels challenging, look for small ways to incorporate moments of presence and awareness into your work routine. Each mindful moment, no matter how brief, is a step on your journey towards becoming a more mindful professional.

Finally, trust in your own capacity for growth and transformation. The journey of mindfulness is deeply personal, and you are the expert on your own experience. As you continue to explore and refine your practice, have confidence in your ability to cultivate greater presence, clarity, and resilience in your professional life. Your commitment to this journey is a powerful investment in your well-being and effectiveness as a professional.

CHAPTER 12: THE MINDFUL PROFESSIONAL: PUTTING IT ALL TOGETHER

As we reach the final chapter of our exploration into mindfulness for the busy professional, it's time to step back and view the bigger picture. Throughout this book, we've delved into various aspects of mindfulness and how they can be applied to enhance our professional lives. Now, let's bring all these pieces together to create a holistic view of what it means to be a truly mindful professional.

The journey we've undertaken in this book reflects the multifaceted nature of mindfulness itself. We've seen how mindfulness isn't just a single practice or technique, but a way of approaching our work and life with greater awareness, intention, and presence. This comprehensive approach to mindfulness in the professional context recognizes that our work lives are complex and multidimensional, requiring a toolkit of practices that can be applied in various situations.

Moreover, we've explored how mindfulness can be both a formal practice, such as dedicated meditation sessions, and an informal one, integrated into our daily work activities. This dual approach allows for the flexibility needed to incorporate mindfulness into even the busiest professional schedules, making it accessible and practical for professionals across different fields and roles.

To begin, let's recap the key mindfulness techniques we've explored. We started with the foundation of mindful breathing, learning how to use our breath as an anchor to the present moment. We then moved on to body awareness, discovering how tuning into our physical sensations can ground us and provide valuable insights. We explored mindful eating, communication, and time management, learning how to bring presence and intention to these everyday activities.

Mindful breathing serves as the cornerstone of many mindfulness practices. By focusing on our breath, we create a point of stability amidst the chaos of our workday. This simple yet powerful technique can be used in various professional contexts - before important meetings, during stressful situations, or as a way to transition between tasks. The beauty of breath awareness is its accessibility; our breath is always with us, providing a constant opportunity for mindfulness.

Body awareness builds on this foundation, extending our mindfulness practice to include our physical sensations. In a professional context, this can be particularly valuable for recognizing and addressing stress before it becomes overwhelming. By tuning into our body, we can detect early signs of tension or fatigue, allowing us to take proactive steps to maintain our well-being and productivity.

We delved into more advanced topics such as mindful decision-making and leadership, seeing how mindfulness can enhance our cognitive abilities and interpersonal skills. We also addressed the challenges of maintaining mindfulness in our digital age, exploring strategies for using technology mindfully. Finally, we looked at how to create a personalized mindfulness practice that fits into the unique demands of your professional life.

Mindful decision-making represents a significant application of mindfulness in the professional realm. By bringing greater awareness to our thought processes and emotional states, we can make clearer, more balanced decisions. This is particularly crucial in leadership roles, where decisions can have far-reaching impacts on teams and organizations.

The exploration of mindful leadership highlighted how mindfulness can transform not just individual performance, but also team dynamics and organizational culture. Mindful leaders tend to be more emotionally intelligent, better able to navigate complex interpersonal situations, and more effective at inspiring and motivating their teams. This ripple effect of mindfulness from the individual to the collective level underscores its potential for widespread positive impact in professional settings.

Creating a mindful daily routine is about weaving these various techniques and principles into the fabric of your workday. This doesn't mean adding hours of meditation to your already packed schedule. Instead, it's about finding small ways to inject mindfulness into your existing routine.

The key to creating a sustainable mindful routine is integration rather than addition. By finding ways to incorporate mindfulness into activities you're already doing, you make it a natural part of your day rather than another task on your to-do list. This approach recognizes the realities of busy professional life while still allowing for the cultivation of mindfulness.

You might start your day with a few minutes of mindful breathing before you get out of bed, setting an intention for the day ahead. As you commute to work, whether by car, public transport, or on foot, use this time for a mindful check-in, noticing your thoughts and feelings without judgment.

This morning routine sets a mindful tone for the day, helping you start work with a sense of calm and focus. The commute, often seen as lost time, becomes an opportunity for mindfulness practice. Whether you're driving, walking, or using public transport, you can use this time to center yourself and prepare mentally for the day ahead.

At work, consider starting each meeting with a moment of collective breath awareness, helping everyone to center themselves and be more present for the discussion. Use transitions between tasks as opportunities for brief mindfulness breaks - perhaps a minute of mindful breathing or a quick body scan.

Introducing mindfulness into meetings can significantly improve their quality and productivity. A brief moment of collective awareness at the start of a meeting can help participants transition from their previous tasks and become more fully present. This can lead to more focused discussions, better listening, and more creative problem-solving.

During lunch, practice mindful eating, even if only for the first few bites. As you interact with colleagues, bring mindful communication principles into play, really listening and speaking with intention. When you find yourself getting stressed or overwhelmed, use the STOP technique (Stop, Take a breath, Observe, Proceed) to reset.

Mindful eating provides a valuable opportunity to step away from work mentally and recharge. Even if you can't dedicate your entire lunch break to mindful eating, focusing on the first few bites can help you transition into a more present state. This midday reset can improve your focus and productivity for the afternoon ahead.

End your workday with a mindful transition ritual - perhaps a short meditation or a mindful walk - to help you shift from work mode to personal time. In the evening, try a longer body scan or loving-kindness meditation to unwind and cultivate positive emotions.

The transition from work to personal time is crucial for maintaining work-life balance. A mindful transition ritual can help you leave work stress behind and be more fully present in your personal life. This not only benefits your well-being but also allows you to return to work the next day feeling refreshed and recharged.

Remember, the goal isn't to be mindful every second of the day, but to sprinkle moments of mindfulness throughout your routine, gradually building your capacity for presence and awareness.

This approach to mindfulness recognizes that perfection is not the aim. It's about progress, not perfection. By incorporating small moments of mindfulness throughout your day, you gradually build your capacity for presence and awareness. Over time, these small practices can lead to significant shifts in your overall mindset and approach to work.

Mindfulness can play a crucial role in career development and job satisfaction. As you become more mindful, you may find that you gain greater clarity about your professional goals and values. You might become more aware of which aspects of your work truly energize you and which drain you. This self-awareness can guide you in making more aligned career choices and in shaping your current role to better suit your strengths and interests.

The enhanced self-awareness that comes from mindfulness practice can be transformative for career development. It allows you to see more clearly what truly motivates and fulfills you professionally. This clarity can guide you in making career decisions that align with your authentic self, leading to greater job satisfaction and overall life satisfaction.

Moreover, mindfulness can help you navigate the inevitable challenges and uncertainties of career development. By cultivating a non-judgmental, accepting attitude towards your experiences, you can approach career setbacks or transitions with greater resilience and openness to learning.

Mindfulness can also enhance your ability to learn and grow professionally. By being more present and focused, you can absorb new information more effectively. The non-judgmental awareness cultivated in mindfulness practice can help you approach challenges and setbacks with curiosity rather than frustration, turning them into valuable learning experiences.

In the rapidly evolving modern workplace, the ability to learn continuously and adapt to new situations is crucial. Mindfulness supports this by enhancing your ability to stay present and engaged in learning experiences. Whether you're attending a training session, learning a new skill, or adapting to a new role, mindfulness can help you approach these situations with an open, curious mindset.

Furthermore, the improved focus that comes from mindfulness practice can enhance your ability to retain and apply new information. By training your mind to stay present and resist distractions, you can engage more deeply with learning materials and experiences, leading to more effective professional development.

Moreover, the emotional intelligence developed through mindfulness practice can significantly boost your professional relationships and leadership capabilities. As you become more attuned to your own emotions and those of others, you'll likely find that you're better able to navigate complex interpersonal dynamics, resolve conflicts, and inspire and motivate your team.

Emotional intelligence is increasingly recognized as a key factor in professional success, particularly in leadership roles. Mindfulness cultivates the self-awareness and self-regulation that are foundational to emotional intelligence. As you become more aware of your own emotional states and reactions, you're better able to manage them effectively in professional situations.

This enhanced emotional intelligence also extends to your interactions with others. Mindfulness can improve your ability to pick up on subtle emotional cues from colleagues, clients, or team members. This heightened awareness allows for more empathetic and effective communication, leading to stronger professional relationships and more successful collaborations.

The ripple effect of your mindfulness practice extends far beyond your own experience. As you become more mindful, you may notice changes in how others respond to you. Your increased presence and calm can have a contagious effect, positively influencing the overall atmosphere of your workplace. Your mindful communication may inspire others to listen more deeply and speak more thoughtfully. Your ability to stay composed under pressure might help your team navigate stressful situations more effectively.

This ripple effect highlights the interconnected nature of our professional environments. When one person begins to operate from a place of greater mindfulness, it can shift the dynamics of entire teams or departments. Your calm presence in a stressful meeting might help others remain centered. Your thoughtful, mindful communication might inspire colleagues to communicate more effectively.

Over time, these individual acts of mindfulness can contribute to a more positive and productive work culture. Stress levels may decrease, collaboration may improve, and the overall quality of work may increase. This demonstrates how personal mindfulness practice can have far-reaching effects beyond individual well-being and performance.

Furthermore, as you model mindful behavior, you may find that others become curious about your approach. This can create opportunities to share mindfulness practices with colleagues, potentially catalyzing a shift towards a more mindful organizational culture.

As mindfulness becomes more visible in your workplace through your actions and their effects, you may find colleagues expressing interest in your approach. This curiosity provides an opportunity to share the benefits of mindfulness more explicitly. You might consider leading short mindfulness exercises at the start of meetings, offering lunchtime meditation sessions, or simply discussing your practice with interested coworkers.

However, it's important to approach this sharing with sensitivity and respect for others' perspectives. Not everyone may be open to mindfulness practices, and that's okay. The goal is to make mindfulness available and accessible to those who are interested, not to impose it on others.

Looking to the future, workplace mindfulness is a trend that shows no signs of slowing down. More and more organizations are recognizing the benefits of mindfulness for employee well-being, productivity, and innovation. We're likely to see an increase in workplace mindfulness programs, mindfulness-based leadership development, and the integration of mindfulness principles into organizational structures and processes.

The growing recognition of mindfulness in professional settings reflects a broader shift in how we understand productivity and success in the workplace. There's an increasing awareness that sustainable high performance requires more than just hard work – it requires a holistic approach that includes mental and emotional well-being.

As this trend continues, we may see mindfulness becoming a more integral part of professional development and organizational strategy. Companies might invest in mindfulness training as part of their employee development programs. Leadership models may evolve to incorporate mindfulness principles. Workplace design might shift to include spaces dedicated to mindfulness practice.

At the same time, as our work environments continue to evolve, particularly with the rise of remote and hybrid work models, the ability to maintain mindfulness amidst digital distractions will become increasingly crucial. We may see the development of new technologies designed to support mindfulness in virtual work environments.

The shift towards remote and hybrid work presents both challenges and opportunities for mindfulness practice. On one hand, working from home can provide more flexibility for incorporating mindfulness into the workday. On the other hand, the blurring of work and personal life boundaries and the increase in digital communication can make it more challenging to stay present and focused.

Future developments in workplace mindfulness may include new technologies specifically designed to support mindfulness in digital environments. This might include apps that provide mindful breaks during virtual meetings, virtual reality meditation spaces, or AI-powered mindfulness assistants that offer personalized mindfulness prompts throughout the workday. The mindful professional of the future will likely need to be adept at navigating both physical and virtual work spaces with presence and intention. They'll need to balance the benefits of connectivity with the need for focused work and digital boundaries. They'll need to cultivate resilience and adaptability to thrive in rapidly changing work environments.

This evolving landscape of work requires a new set of skills, with mindfulness at their core. The ability to maintain focus and presence amidst digital distractions, to connect authentically with colleagues in virtual spaces, and to manage the boundaries between work and personal life will be crucial. Mindfulness provides a foundation for developing these skills, offering techniques for staying grounded and centered regardless of external circumstances.

Moreover, as the pace of change in the professional world continues to accelerate, the ability to adapt and remain resilient will be increasingly valuable. Mindfulness cultivates a flexible, open mindset that can help professionals navigate uncertainty and change with greater ease. It provides tools for managing the stress and anxiety that often accompany rapid change, allowing professionals to remain effective and balanced even in turbulent times.

As we conclude this book, remember that becoming a mindful professional is not about reaching a final destination. It's an ongoing journey of growth, learning, and self-discovery. There will be days when mindfulness comes easily, and others when it feels challenging. The key is to approach each day, each task, each interaction with renewed intention and curiosity.

The journey of mindfulness is lifelong, with each day offering new opportunities for practice and growth. Some days, you may find yourself naturally embodying the principles of mindfulness in your work. Other days, you might struggle to stay present and centered. Both experiences are part of the journey, offering valuable lessons and opportunities for deepening your practice.

Remember that mindfulness is not about achieving a state of perpetual calm or eliminating all stress from your work life. It's about developing the capacity to be with whatever arises in your professional life with greater awareness and equanimity. It's about cultivating the ability to respond thoughtfully rather than react automatically to the challenges and opportunities you encounter.

Your mindfulness practice is a powerful tool for enhancing your professional life, but its benefits extend far beyond the workplace. As you continue to cultivate mindfulness, you may find that it transforms not just how you work, but how you live. It can lead to greater overall well-being, more fulfilling relationships, and a deeper sense of purpose and meaning in all aspects of your life.

The skills and awareness you develop through mindfulness practice at work naturally spill over into your personal life. You may find that you're more present with family and friends, more able to enjoy leisure time without worrying about work, and more in tune with your own needs and values. This integration of mindfulness across all areas of life can lead to a greater sense of balance and fulfillment.

Moreover, as you continue to deepen your mindfulness practice, you may find that it leads to profound shifts in your perspective on work and life. You might discover a renewed sense of purpose in your career, or find new ways to align your work with your personal values. You may develop a greater appreciation for the interconnectedness of all aspects of your life, seeing how your professional growth contributes to your personal development and vice versa.

So, as you close this book and return to your professional life, carry with you the practices and principles we've explored. Let them guide you towards a more mindful, balanced, and fulfilling career. And remember, each breath, each moment of awareness, is an opportunity to begin anew on this path of mindful professionalism. Your journey continues, one mindful moment at a time.

As you move forward, consider how you can continue to nurture and expand your mindfulness practice. Perhaps you'll seek out additional resources, join a mindfulness group, or even consider becoming a mindfulness advocate in your workplace. Whatever path you choose, trust in your ability to bring greater awareness, intentionality, and presence to your professional life.

Remember that your mindfulness journey is unique to you. While the principles and practices we've explored are universal, how you apply them in your specific work context will be personal to you. Be open to experimenting, adapting, and finding what works best for you. And above all, approach your practice with patience, self-compassion, and a sense of curiosity about what each new day might bring.

As you continue on this path of mindful professionalism, know that you are part of a growing movement of individuals bringing greater awareness and intentionality to the workplace. Your commitment to mindfulness not only benefits you but contributes to a broader shift towards more conscious, compassionate, and effective ways of working. Each mindful moment you create ripples out, influencing your colleagues, your organization, and ultimately, the larger professional world. Your journey as a mindful professional is both a personal path of growth and a contribution to positive change in the working world.

www.ingramcontent.com/pod-product-compliance
Lightning Source LLC
Chambersburg PA
CBHW071059240526
45471CB00016B/2163